S. SANDS

S. SANDS

NO MORE VICTIMS

By

S. Sands

**ONE MAN'S JOURNEY
INTO SEXUAL
OFFENDING AND
RECOVERY**

Published by

KJ Nivin

kjnivin@yahoo.com

Virginia Beach, VA 23451

No More Victims

One Man's Journey into

Sexual Offending and Recovery

ISBN: 1460926730
EAN-13: 9781460926734

NO MORE VICTIMS

S. SANDS

Disclaimer

No More Victims is not intended to replace professional counseling or professional medical help. The sole intention of *No More Victims* is to bring awareness to and assist in identification of behaviors that may lead to sexual abuse / offending of minors or adults. There are no guarantees implied or otherwise stated herein. It is possible that compulsive behavior and/or addictive sexual behavior may be arrested and managed. It may be necessary to seek professional help in the way of counseling and/or 12 Step Programs as well as legal advice.

No More Victims has no affiliation with any 12 Step organizations. These organizations are autonomous and are not affiliated with any outside entities. Nor does it have affiliation with the professional counseling industry, penal systems, or government organizations. This book is the experience, strength, and hope of S. Sands (pseudonym), who shares his struggles with and recovery from being a sexual offender.

He has been able to live a more normal life by following some important guidelines and by making life changes. He is sharing this in hopes that others may benefit by his efforts.

Foreword

What I have presented herein represents my path in life that led me to my addictive sexual behavior and eventual sexual offending. It is a long path from teenage inappropriate behavior to finally acting out with my two victims when in my 60's. It further represents my path to understanding the gravity of my offending behavior and the forces I allowed to take control of my life. In no way does it excuse my behavior or lessen both the short and long term traumas that my victims have experienced and that will continue to have an impact on their lives.

If I could turn back the clock, I certainly would. I know to say "I'm sorry" to my victims falls far short of what is needed to help them understand that what happened was not their fault. I take full responsibility for my actions. There is nothing I can do to take away what I have done. The only way I know how to show any more remorse is to go forward with my life, acknowledge my mistakes, and create "No More Victims."

I can only hope my victims, after receiving therapy, are able to go on with their lives and hold their heads up high. My purpose in writing what I have is that it might help someone else seek help before they go down the same path I did. If what I have written helps even one person change the negative direction of their life, then my effort will have been worth it. It will be a small contribution in making amends for what I did.

NO MORE VICTIMS

Table of Contents

Acknowledgments

On one of my early visits to my therapist upon release on parole, he asked that I write an autobiographical sketch of my sexual background. I did so and his comment was, "That's a good first chapter." Eleven additional chapters later, I finally stopped. I thank Mr. David Rossetti, LCSW-R, for his suggestions and encouragement to dig deeper that made this small but important book possible. It is also necessary to credit my initial editor, Euan Bear, with some of the changes I made at her suggestion. We didn't see eye to eye on the direction I was taking the book so we parted ways. But her input was valued.

Further, I also thank Pastors John and Bill; my two VA therapists; my niece, my high school classmate Dr. Ron, and KJ Nivin for their encouragement and suggestions. It is also necessary to thank the Sex Offender Program professional staff at the Oneida Correctional Facility for their opening my eyes to my erroneous thoughts, feelings, and behaviors.

Last, but by no means least, I thank my wife for putting up with my negative actions over the years and for allowing me to bare my soul to put this together. I can only hope my efforts will help someone stop and think before they go down the same road as I (or, perhaps, do it again).

Chapter 1

In the Beginning...

"The major question is: 'Why did I commit the crime I did? The major goal is: 'To make sure to get the help I need so that I never commit another sex crime again.'"

Robert E. Longo, et al

Introduction

You are reading this book, more than likely, because someone has recommended it. They may be concerned about the direction your life is taking or has taken. Your life appears to center around thoughts of sex and acting on those thoughts in various ways—some legal; others not or very questionable. This book is about my life's journey and how it led to my eventual sexual offending. It is my hope that you may see some of yourself in my misguided sexual development. By so doing, take in and use in your own life some of the new perspectives I had to learn the hard way and change your direction before it is too late—or too late again.

It is a story of how I, a then 62-year old man, husband, father and grandfather, went from being active in his church and other positive activities in his community and subscribing to all their positive ideals, became a person scorned and a threat to the community he had loved and served. This evolution posed a question I had to ask myself over and over again, "How the heck did I get myself in this mess?" How could I, at such an age, have sexually offended a 16-year old girl and a 12-year old girl? I pled guilty to one count each of sodomy and rape third, felonies, against a 16-year old female, and acting in a manner injurious to a minor, a misdemeanor, against a 12-year old female—a family member! I had to find an explanation. In order to prevent future occurrences, I needed to find the root causes of my misguided sexual thoughts, feelings, and behaviors that led to my choice to inappropriately act.

One point I need to emphasize is that despite my finding what I felt to be the "root causes" of my sexual offending, they are neither reasons nor justification for doing so; and certainly in no way are they any attempt to lessen the impact of my actions on my victims and extended victims. I, as an educated adult, ultimately

made the decision to sexually offend and am totally responsible for the results of my actions.

What I found on my journey was that I was not alone—there were more out there like me who had similar inappropriate sexual thoughts/feelings/behaviors. But that is no excuse for my behaviors. It only points out the gravity of the problem of sexual abuse/offending. In my journey to find those roots, I am only defining my trip as I look back at it. In no way am I intentionally justifying or rationalizing my actions. I found I harbored a number of negative sexual misconceptions and insecurities. Finding the root causes would, I hoped, help me to see why and how I offended and lead me on the path to understanding the gravity of what I did. Due to my age at the time of the start of my primary inappropriate acting out (I was about 58), I found it helpful to break my life down into smaller periods of time to see how the development progressed. Hopefully you, the reader, will not have to look back that far.

It is also my hope that sharing my story, though there are many variations, along with the succeeding chapters that helped me gain understanding, will help you and others see through my eyes and my experience a path you do not really want, or need, to travel.

In order to get an understanding as to my own sexual offending, I had to use the analogy of one of my Sex Offender Program counselors. He likened the process to peeling an onion. I had to take one layer of my life at a time and look at it thoroughly—examining my thoughts, feelings, and behaviors.

The Evolution Begins

I was 8. My older brother was 16. I remember playing in our living room when my father took my brother into my parent's bedroom. I wanted to go with him, but my mother said, "No, your time will come." My "time," which I later assumed was the usual father-son "talk" about sex, didn't come for my father passed away shortly after my 11th birthday. Soon after the call came about my father's death, my aunt told me I was now the "man" of the house (as my older brother was away in the Army)—I hardly knew what it was to be a boy yet. A leading authority on sexual dysfunction explained how that event, coupled with my father having been gone during a large part of WWII, could have had an impact on me by zmy viewing it as a form abandonment—though I don't remember consciously thinking of those events in that way. Sure, I had other male role models that in various ways filled the void left by my father's earlier absence and later death; but it was not their place to give me "the talk." And I didn't know how to ask, even if they had been willing. There was no sex education in schools at that time either—or at least not formal education.

The Early Years

So, how did I learn about sex? In my teens from peers, from pornography, from being a "Peeping Tom," and from occasionally exposing myself to little girls in hopes they would show me theirs. Watching girls develop and using pornography aroused me, but I really didn't understand why. I recall having what seemed a permanent erection during my high school days. Just being around girls seemed to peak my little understood sexual nature. I did very little dating, as I was extremely shy. I masturbated but never remember ejaculating. Instead, I usually wound up with a swollen penis. Later, my brother told me of his sexual exploits, including those with various female relatives, and asked me when I was around 16 or 17 if I had gotten any of that "strange stuff" as he called it. Not wanting to sound like I wasn't with it, I responded "yes," and that was the extent of his direct sexual influence—except for the sexually explicit magazines he kept at his house which I often looked at when visiting.

"First, sex addicts often begin sexually compulsive behavior early in life," says Dr. Patrick Carnes, in his second book on sexual addiction, **Don't Call It Love— Recovery from Sexual Addiction**[5]. It was a book I quickly identified with. But don't let the word "addiction" stop you from reading further. The subject is relevant to all who have sexually obsessed, sexually abused/offended, or may have the capacity or inclination (due to one's thoughts, feelings, and behaviors regarding sex) to do so.

But what did I really learn beyond the female anatomy--nothing. What I was doing is what is referred to as an escalating sequence of behaviors that can, and did, lead to more serious sexual behavior. Therein lie the "seeds" of my sexual misconduct—and then years of allowing layer after layer of "fertilizer" (continued use of pornographic material) to build up to help those seeds grow—eventually leading to my addiction and inappropriate acting out. "The human mind is like a fertile ground where seeds are continually being planted," said Don Miguel Ruiz, in his book, **The Four Agreements**[3]. He went on to say, "The seeds are opinions, ideas, and concepts." We pick the seeds up all the time and don't always sort them out as to what is a good or bad seed before they become planted and cultivated in our minds. It is important, therefore, to examine one's "seeds" and "fertilizer" regarding sexual issues and ask the vital question, "Where are they leading me?" before life gets out of control. Throughout the book, "seeds" and "fertilizer" are the groundwork for what I refer to as thoughts, feelings, and behaviors.. But let's get further into my "evolution."

The Mid Years

I joined the Navy when I was 19. Prior to my enlistment, I had no direct sexual experience other than as previously noted. During my first Navy deployment to the western Pacific, a trip to Japan resulted in my first sexual encounter, which was with a young Japanese prostitute. Despite her supposed experience, I do not remember ejaculating even then. The feeling that eventually fueled my later addiction was still a mystery to me. I did not experience intercourse again until I married some five years after my first sexual experience despite two more western Pacific deployments. Nor was I into masturbation considering my earlier negative results. I was also haunted by my religious upbringing that gave me the impression that anything sexual was wrong outside of marriage and was consumed by guilt over what I had done on my first deployment. Consciously, I can't remember that my church had anything to do with teaching me the right or wrong of sex. I only assumed it was one of those things that one feels must be wrong because proper, positive sexual information seemed so secretive.

One of the primary shapers of my distorted thoughts regarding sex was, as noted earlier, pornography. On the return trip from my first deployment, I was introduced to what was referred to as "training flics." These "flics" were, in fact, graphically sexual in content and I became drawn to them despite my feelings as to the right or wrong of sex. Two more deployments helped further in developing my sexual outlook by increasing use of those "flics" and other forms of pornography. One point stands out that I'm sure affected my eventual sexual attitude toward women was that the women were portrayed as enjoying sex and even initiating it. I took this in and over time made two conclusions: (1) women wanted and enjoyed sex and (2) women were to sexually please men. Listening to the "exploits" of my peers seemed to reinforce that viewpoint. Regular movies, TV programs, and commercials—both TV and print—increasingly emphasized sex in a carefree manner.

When I married my first wife, my feelings toward women and sex were firmly in place. Sure, I loved her, or at least what I considered love. She was 15 when I met her and I was 23. We married a week after her 17th birthday. She was, as far as I could tell, as sexually naïve as I was—but I had my pre-conceived notion of her role in the sexual aspect of marriage. Among other things, I consider my sexual attitude as one of the reasons for the marriage breakup. We did not discuss sex—I simply expected her to be available and like it as the women in my "training film" and other pornographic sources appeared to do. I was, or thought I was, getting my perceived sexual needs/wants met. Again, it never occurred to me to consider a woman's feelings.

I was faithful for about the first six years of our 8-year marriage—though I will admit my eyes, and thoughts, did wander. It wasn't until I found out that my wife was cheating on me that my attitude towards sex, and women in general, hit rock bottom. We separated and I started looking for female companionship for the sole purpose of sexual fulfillment—my sexual fulfillment. I tried to pick up women wherever and whenever the opportunity presented itself. I didn't take into account, when I had a sexual encounter, what the woman was feeling. All I cared about was how I felt—the rush I got that seemed to take away whatever stress I was feeling, if any. All my earlier sexual encounters were age appropriate, though not necessarily ethically appropriate, until my offending behavior, with one exception, which I will mention later. It steadily became an obsession to find sexual relief. I began using more pornography and masturbation to provide sexual relief when a female partner could not be found. Such actions continued until I remarried.

Never in my wildest dreams would I have thought that I could be seduced by and addicted to that feeling of sexual release—or to anything else for that matter. After the "sexual revolution" of the 60's (love = sex; make love; not war), I began referring to myself as sexually amoral—if it felt good, why not do it—and that included using more and more pornographic material for the purpose of sexual excitement leading to frequent masturbation. In sexual relationships, whether I was single or married or my partners were single or married made no difference to me. Although love, as I interpreted it, was a factor with a couple of my partners, it was not a prime criterion to answer my urges. Although love may eventually lead to sex, just plain sex rarely leads to love. There are many dimensions to a proper, positive sexual relationship that I had never heard of until after I offended; for true love should encompass such personal dimensions as spiritual, emotional, physical, psychological, and ethical realms—not just sexual compatibility. But I rebelled against societal norms. I was in control of my life—or so I thought—and my perceived sexual needs/wants were important to me.

With my second wife, sex was a big part of our early marriage and seemingly satisfying to the both of us. However, after a few years, it became less satisfying to me for I felt too much work was involved in satisfying my wife. Remember, sex was about <u>my</u> satisfaction. Despite the faithfulness of my wife, I started looking for extra-marital affairs and once again resorted to pornography to help settle my urges when a willing partner could not be found. And that continued until my arrest.

The Later Years

Following my retirement from the service, as I became more and more actively involved in my church and community, I found that doing these things helped me to avoid thinking about what I was doing in regards to sex. I simply didn't take time to be me, or rather, to figure out who "me" was. It wasn't until after I offended and sought help that I was diagnosed with a form of depression. Among other things, keeping busy can be a sign of depression—and depression in one form or another is often a part of those who sexually offend. It is that "down" feeling that seeks relief. I was busy "doing" instead of facing my sexual issues. I took the position that, "Okay, I do all these positive things in my life and they far outweigh any wrongs that I may be doing." In that way, I was able to continually justify to myself my sexual behavior. Wrong! When I was finally caused to come face-to-face with the realization of all the lives that got hurt or negatively affected in some way by my inappropriate sexual behavior, it rapidly wiped out any good that I had done.

It is necessary to digress at this point. Why did I gravitate to young girls? Perhaps it is because I felt I could mold them into what I wanted. Their developing bodies intrigued me. I look at my manipulation and use of my two underage victims as those I could control and "teach" them how to please a man. With my ex-wife, sexual contact in the form of caressing started fairly early in our relationship. Intercourse did not happen until we married. Not that I didn't try, but again, my shyness held me back.

One of the things I required of a potential sex partner was their willingness. If I had to "work" at obtaining sex, it diminished my enthusiasm and pleasure. I feared rejection as well if I didn't "perform" to someone's expectations. Again, all my sex partners prior to my arrest had been age appropriate until my son asked us to allow a friend of his, an emancipated 16-year old girl, to live with us. I attempted to fondle her the first night in the house. She told her then boy friend who confronted and warned me to not let it happen again. A few years later, and several years after my son married the girl we had taken in (and was at that time separated from her), I had consensual intercourse with her.

A new dimension was added to my considering young girls for sexual conquest. My brother and I were facing our mortality. Both our father and his brother died at age 58. Though my brother had already passed that milestone, it was still an issue with me. As I approached and surpassed 58, I wanted to feel young (or at least act young) and be accepted by young people. When my brother unexpectedly died at 70, the mortality issue really hit home. A sort of "live for today for tomorrow you may die" attitude, apparently already in place, further enhanced my inappropriate sexual mindset—get it while you are able.

During my participation in the required Sex Offender Program while incarcerated, my counselor at that time, in critiquing one of my presentations, made the comment that I "degraded and humiliated women." "Where did that come from?" I said to myself. I never considered my actions that low. That evening I called my wife and told her what the counselor said. I was stunned! Her response, "I could have told you that." She then outlined some of my words and actions and how they belittled her—and had been noticed by others. I had been both verbally and psychologically abusive to her. Besides being incarcerated, those words became my biggest wake up call. From that point on, I had to take a long hard look at how my thoughts, feelings, and behaviors towards women had been played out. Perhaps my counselors words were a little on the strong side, but I had to admit, with his comment and my wife's assent, I agreed with the basis of the assessment. What an eye opener!

On to Recovery

My life is definitely different, as I said in the beginning, and so it is with my victims, and will be that way for the rest of our lives. But I think I can live with that for I am blessed to have an understanding, compassionate, forgiving, and loving wife. But there is no doubt that I hurt her deeply and have had to work hard at rebuilding a loving and trusting relationship—and it will be a continual work in progress. How others react to living next to or be near a registered sex offender will be mixed. Only time and my positive behavior from here on will tell. My sexual attitude and eventual addiction <u>did not happen overnight</u>. It took a long time to develop. It also takes time to come to grips with one's past sexual thoughts, feelings, and behaviors and replace them with more appropriate ones. The time can vary from person to person.

Can sexual addiction or obsessive pre-occupation with sex be cured? No more than can alcoholism or drug addiction or any other addiction or excessive behavior. However, as with other addictions or obsessive conduct, the person must first accept the premise that he/she has a problem. Then it <u>may</u> be controlled through education, counseling, 12-step program participation, and sometimes with the help of medication or a combination of all four. (Recovery will be covered more in Chapter 11.) It is important, therefore, to recognize and understand your thoughts, feelings, and behaviors. Sexual temptations abound—know yourself! Limit your exposure to sexually explicit material. But more importantly, think of what your inappropriate sexual actions will do to a victim, the victim's family, and your family. It is immense!

Now that my life has been revealed—the thoughts, feelings, and behaviors that led to my evolution as a sex offender—where do I go from here? The major question still remains "Why did I commit the crime I did?" I found it difficult to believe how I could have let myself follow such a path. But I did; and the road to recovery will not be, and has not been, easy. Now, however, I need to make sure I put into practice the lessons I have learned and continue to get the help I need to further my understanding so I never commit another sex crime.

Although it is easy to feel sorry for oneself for circumstances in which they may find themselves, the real sufferers are those left behind: Spouses, children, and parents, and other family members of both victim and offender and friends who are left to pick up the pieces of their lives that the sex offender's actions disrupted. There is no such thing as only one person being affected by the inappropriate actions of another when it comes to sexual offending.

During the incarceration of a sex offender, at least in New York State and several others, in order to be released on parole, it is considered necessary to take and satisfactorily complete a minimum six month Sex Offender Training Program. The program I attended consisted of eight educational modules, a detailed presentation of the acceptance of responsibility for the various acts done to the victims as well as the various harms caused the victim and extended victims, a detailed sexual offending cycle and relapse prevention plan (these will be explained in later chapters). Such presentations are done before one's peers in the program and a civilian counselor, who was alluded to earlier, who are free to critique (for or against) any aspect of the presentations.

Note: One thing that was difficult to deal with in the Sex Offender Program was having to daily describe over and over again what we did to our victim(s) in clinical terms (proper bodily parts) not by slang/street terms. Again, by doing so, it made our offending behavior more real—that it actually involved another human being.

The eight modules were:

Sexual Offending	Your Victim(s)
Pre-Abuse	Learned Behavior
Relapse Prevention	Sexual Offending Cycle
Grooming	Responsibility/Empathy

I added four additional ones: "In the Beginning"— how it all started; I also added "Defense Mechanisms" to "Responsibility" and made "Empathy" a separate chapter. Finally I included "Recovery"—getting one's life back on track and "No More Victims"—a summary on how not to create any more victims. I'll summarize the contents of the modules in the succeeding chapters for I feel the information presented, which helped me understand the gravity of my inappropriate thoughts, feelings, and behaviors, and re-direct them in more positive ways, will help you, the reader, in the same way. But first it is essential to point out that "if you remain as you are and don't understand why you committed your crime(s) [or obsessive sexual behavior], statistics, experience, and history indicate that you will more than likely go out and commit other crimes [or continue obsessive sexual behavior]..." [7]   "Hope and willpower alone are not enough to stop you from offending or re-offending. You must also have the tools and know-ledge that treatment can offer you;" [7] and the <u>desire</u> to apply them to your life. The tools and knowledge will be explained in later chapters.

As much as I hate to admit it, going to prison probably saved my life. The way I was going I'm sure my behaviors would have gotten worse. That seemed to leave me with two possibilities as I look back: 1) suicide for bringing about such great shame or 2) facing many more years of incarceration that neither I nor my family could have handled. The opportunity to take the Sex Offender Program opened my eyes to the erroneous thoughts, feelings, and behaviors that had been driving me to sexually offend.

Special Note: **If in referring to my victims, and any references to sexual material, has a negative sexual effect on you, then they just might be cause for concern regarding your sexual attitude. They can be considered "Triggers," those things that may set you off on a course to sexually abuse/offend and need to be avoided as much as possible.**

Sexual Addiction

It is important at this point to briefly introduce the concept of sexual addiction as it has already been referred to and will be again. I didn't understand it. I didn't see how someone could be addicted to anything, let alone something as natural as sex. "Sexual addiction is the term commonly used to describe sexual obsession. A sex addict is willing to be destructive to self and others, even breaking the law if necessary, to achieve sexual pleasure."[1] I didn't use drugs, I had quit smoking some thirty years before I offended, considered myself a social drinker (usually three was my limit), didn't gamble or do any of the "normal" things people become addicted to. For that matter, I felt people who became addicted were weak. Why couldn't they just limit their drinking or stop as I did with smoking? I did not realize the powerful hold addiction could have on someone—on me. Now I know! Now I understand!

It is also necessary to clarify that all sex offenders are not sex addicts; but it is safer to say that most sex addicts, with unchecked behavior, are more than likely to be or to become sexual offenders. Dr. Carnes, notes in his book, **Out of the Shadows— Understanding Sexual Addiction[4],** that "Sexual addiction has been described as 'the athlete's foot of the mind.' It never goes away. It always is asking to be scratched, promising relief. To scratch, however, is to cause pain and intensify the itch." He goes on to say, "Only the individual addict knows the shame of living a double life—the real world and the addict's world." **My world!** Hopefully, not yours.

Chapter 2

Sexual Offending

"Sexual assault [offending] is forced or tricked sexual contact which need not but can involve touching."
Barbara K. Swartz, PhD
Gregory M. S. Canfield, MSW

Guilty! Life as I knew it was over—words that I heard over and over again for over five years while incarcerated and on parole for the sexual offences I mentioned in Chapter 1. And truer words could not be spoken.

What is sexual offending? The question will be covered as well in succeeding chapters, but simply stated, it is taking inappropriate sexual liberties towards another person against their will (and that includes those under the age of consent or lacking the mental and/or physical ability to give consent) not what you may think they want. The act of sexual offending begs the question—WHY?

Why would we want to violate someone's personal space when we wouldn't want it done to us? Why do we cause shame and embarrassment to others as well as ourselves? One of the primary reasons a person becomes a sex offender/abuser is that he/she thinks of him/herself only, though they seldom acknowledge that point. As sex offenders/abusers, we are quick to pass the blame for our actions to persons, places, or things; e.g., we were sexually offended or abused as a child is often an excuse given for inappropriate sexual behavior. The only blame that can stand up is to blame ourselves for not considering the feelings of others when <u>choosing</u> to abuse/offend someone.

There are probably as many reasons for sexual offending as there are offenders. Each has his own story. For me it was a craving for the attention of young girls—I dreaded getting and looking old; I had a need to control; I thought I could get away with it; and my addiction to the sexual release all contributed to my eventual sexual offending. Lack of empathy (which will be covered in more detail later) and a general disregard for the deepest personal feelings of others also make the list. It is the "me" factor. It is what the offender wants and intends to get whether the other person is willing or not (of legal age, mentally/physically capable or not).

As has been mentioned before, sexual offending does not just happen. If we have excessive sexual thoughts and personal sexual habits, it is usually only a matter of time before physically acting out with someone inappropriately becomes a reality. My mindset became so fixed on what I considered to be my perceived sexual needs (or wants), that in my mind I could make someone become the object of my sexual fantasy. It is a process called objectification which, in effect, turns a person into an object not unlike the alcoholic whose object is the bottle or the drug user whose object is the next fix. We literally dehumanize a person to make them an object of our sexual desire.

Sexual acting out is like a stolen wrapped present. We may symbolically tear apart a person's outer trappings like we attack the wrapping paper on a gift just to get what is inside. Only we may care little for the human being. It is what we think we want for our misplaced sense of pleasure.

Once again it is necessary to emphasize that sexual offending/obsession does not just happen. It is the result of what I have put into a "mathematical" formula:

Thoughts + Feelings + Behavior + Opportunity + (Choice) = Offending/Acting Out

Depending on how long one has developed those sexual thoughts, feelings, and behaviors, the acting out can take days, weeks, months, even years, to happen—or it can happen in a matter of minutes when opportunity becomes available. Regardless of the length of time one dwells on the first three factors of the above "formula," it takes a conscious choice to each of them to move the abuse/offending forward.

Thoughts: Something we have every waking moment. Many we may not be conscious of for they can pop up at the sight, sound, or feel of something familiar or peculiar and disappear just as quickly. Others linger and we may ask ourselves questions about what we have seen, heard, or felt that grabbed our attention. We ponder them and form opinions based on them. We think about how to earn money; what type of employment we would like; what to do for fun. Thoughts, and the feelings and behaviors they can generate, help define who we are as a person. We cannot escape our thoughts but we can learn to control some of them.

41

When we have negative thoughts (those that affect our feelings and make us sad, hurt, or angry, for example), we can replace them with thoughts that make us feel more comfortable. To do so will require retraining our mindset. Certainly there will be events in our lives that bother us and create negative thoughts. The difference is in how we respond to them. If our response causes us (or may cause us) to harm someone (sexual abuse/assault, for example), then that is wrong. That is why we need to be in touch with our thoughts in order to stop those that can potentially cause harm to someone. We need to develop a more positive thought pattern and that may require professional counseling.

Just as my victims needed help to unravel the harm I did to them, we need help to change our harmful thoughts, beliefs, and feelings that produced that harm. **Remember, in sexual abuse/assault, there is always more than one person harmed—in varying degrees.** That idea will be covered in more detail in a later chapter.

My mind was consumed with thinking of ways to meet my perceived sexual "needs"—or, in the words of my Sex Offender counselor, my "sexual wants." I doubt a day went by when I didn't think of with whom, where, and when, my perceived sexual needs/wants would be satisfied. Being in places where there were a lot of females provided me with a veritable smorgasbord of thoughts as well as feelings. They gave me the fodder for my fantasy sexual world.

Feelings: We all have them—from feeling good to feeling sad and many others. And we don't always understand why we feel a particular way and often react to our feelings instead of thinking them out. If our thoughts are often sexual in nature, they are bound to generate sexual feelings. Many negative feelings have tell-tale signs that should warn us that our feelings are headed in the wrong direction: sweating, heart racing, hate, muscles tight, teeth clenched, and in my case, feelings of insecurity (people won't want to work with me, like me, or may give me a difficult time, for example) are just a few of the signs that indicate we may be having negative feelings. The feelings of insecurity I had reduced my effectiveness, in my eyes at least, in both work and volunteer activities. I now feel that seeking sexual gratification gave me a false sense that I was okay—that I was in charge of my life. But like thoughts, harmful feelings can be changed and counseling may be necessary in order to get in touch with negative feelings. I didn't try to get in touch with my feelings. I was, frankly, scared to look at them. I certainly knew something was not right, but kept busy to avoid having to deal with them. Yet at the same time, stressed myself to the point that I mentally cried out for sexual relief, my "drug" of choice. It took the SOP to open my mind to how dominant my thoughts and feelings regarding sex were. Unencumbered by the stresses I put on myself on the outside, I could totally focus my mind toward understanding where I went wrong.

"Many ask how sex can be an addiction [The addiction aspect of sexual offending/abuse will be covered in more detail later.] when no drug is ingested," says Dr. Carnes in **Don't Call It Love**[5]. He goes on to say, "Drugs, in fact, are involved—in the form of naturally occurring peptides such as endorphins which govern the electro-chemical interactions within the brain. These peptides parallel the molecular construction of opiates like morphine, but they are many times more powerful." "A more difficult recovery is one of the prices of getting high on one's brain chemistry." Again, in **Contrary to Love**[2], Dr. Carnes noted that, "Contrary to enjoying sex as a self-affirming source of physical pleasure, the sex addict has learned to rely on sex for comfort from pain, nurturing, or relief from stress, etc, the way an alcoholic relies on alcohol, or a drug addict on drugs." Although I can't deny the pleasurable aspects of sex, I now know I used it as my stress reliever in an inappropriate manner.

Behavior: "Our lives are made up of millions of individual behaviors—many of which we pay little attention to at the time. The choice of certain groups of behaviors often means the difference between success and failure, being in trouble or being helpful, and solving a problem or making it worse. Learning to identify individual behaviors and small groups of behaviors will both help you better understand how you've gotten into this mess in the past and make better choices in the future. If you know how to recognize how problem behaviors start and what they look like for you, you have a much better chance of avoiding them." [8]

As we think sexual thoughts and develop sexual feelings, the next step is usually to act on them. Our behavior may be as innocent as masturbating while viewing pornography either through books, magazines, or videos, or occasionally on the Internet, or it may go much further to the actual violation of another human being. Use of many of the pornographic choices fueled my desire for live contact. "Adult [or any type of] pornography…has the potential to depersonalize and dehumanize sexual relations and refocus sexual behavior solely for the purpose of self-gratification."[21] That is the effect it had on me and goes back to my introduction to pornographic films. It is important to state here that pornography is not a victimless crime. Just because direct human contact may not be part of what is used to cause sexual relief, someone somewhere put themselves in a position, for whatever reason, to be displayed in a sexual manner. I didn't realize, or understand that, until I took the SOP. For the purpose of simplification, future use of the term "pornography" includes all forms of sexual display: movies, strip clubs, adult book stores, etc. Unlike other forms of addiction where the product (alcohol, drugs, etc.) are used up, "The only things 'used up' in the … pornography business are its victims," so said Andrew Vachss in "Let's Fight This Terrible Crime Against Our

Children," an article in **Parade**[13] magazine, February 19, 2006. Worst of all, most pornography gets used over and over again constantly re-victimizing the victims. For those in prison for computer related sexual crimes, it was necessary for them to create a fantasy person and work the program with that person in mind. That included describing the sexual acting out that they would have done had their "victim" been a real person. It was often harder for them to create a victim scenario from an image than those of us who had a real live victim. Use of such material is often part of the escalating sequence of behaviors referred to earlier that can lead to direct sexual abusing/offending. When these three forces built up in me, and opportunity presented itself, I was ready to act out. And with my two victims, they, as with my former daughter-in-law, were in my house, or vehicle, which presented my opportunity—"under my roof, under my control!"

Opportunity: This is the phase where sexual offending can take place. We have thought sexual thoughts, we have had sexual feelings (and it is a most powerful feeling) and perhaps acted out through masturbation or other less invasive methods. We can create that opportunity by taking advantage of innocent children, or those individuals physically or mentally challenged. We can bribe our intended victim(s), threaten them, drug them or ply them with alcohol. Or we can take advantage of anyone simply because we have some advantage over them—education, age, strength, for example. These points will be covered further in Chapter 4. Opportunity happens when we don't rein in our inappropriate thoughts, feelings, and behaviors and put ourselves in a position to act on them—be it school yard, playground, cruising, youth/teen/adult hangouts or wherever our preferred victim type might be found.

Choice: When it comes right down to it, during any of the first four parts of the "equation," we need to become aware that we have two choices 1) not only to act on them but also how that acting out should be done, or 2) not act on them by using thought stopping actions (to be defined in Chapters 9 & 10) that turn us away from acting on the sexual impulses we had.

Despite the fact that I was beginning to develop the fear of getting caught, I could not bring myself to stop my offending behaviors. My internal voice told me to stop but my perceived sexual needs/wants demanded their fulfillment.

Offending/Acting Out: When all of the above factors come together and the choice to act on them is made, the usual result is acting out in one form or another on the sexual urges we have.

Modern societies have laws that define what is right and what is wrong. Good behavior is referred to as *social order*—that as a rule, society can be expected to perform in an orderly and predictable manner. When that doesn't happen, those not following society's norms (laws) then subject themselves to *social control*. In other words, they suffer the legal penalties for going against those norms.

Sex abusers/offenders, therefore, because their actions deviate from what is acceptable by society, need to recognize their unacceptable behavior and work to alter their deviant nature. Call it imprisonment; call it therapy. Whatever condition or name is used, it is an effort to bring those who have deviated from society's expected sexual behavior to an understanding of their inappropriate actions and the impact they have had on others and how to prevent future occurrences.

Prison is where I finally became fully aware of my sexual attitude. It is with great regret that I involved and scarred two innocent lives in my quest for the sexual relief I felt I needed/wanted. That I had to take such a dramatic route was, unfortunately, essential to my future well-being and the well-being of any future victims I may have created had I not received the awareness and therapy I did. "It is common for offenders in therapy to complain that therapy focuses only on the bad stuff. They want to tell their therapists about what is good in their lives [as I did]. While being able to see the good in life is important, you have been using the 'good' sides of yourself as a way of hiding the compartmentalized deviant side. You have to look at your deviant, destructive side clearly and realistically so you can change it."[7] That is what the prison sexual offender program and psych counseling forced me to do.

Another way to look at ourselves in answer to the "Why" question earlier, is as if we were wearing masks—

different masks to cover up different feelings or emotions. The following comes from <u>One Day At A Time (AA)</u>, the February 20th reading:

> "We are often told in the Program [AA] that more will be revealed.' As we are restored to health [normalcy] and become increasingly able to live comfortably in the real world without using chemicals [including our own natural brain chemistry], we begin to see many things in a new light. Many of us have come to realize, for example, that our archenemy, anger, comes disguised in many shapes and colors: intolerance, contempt, snobbishness, rigidity, tension, sarcasm, distrust, anxiety, envy, hatred, cynicism, discontent, self-pity, malice, suspicion, jealousy. 'Do I let my feelings get the best of me? May I recognize that my anger, like a dancer at a masquerade, wears many forms and many faces. May I strip off its several masks and know it for what it is.'
>
> Anger wears a thousand masks."

I can honestly say I wore a mask—a lot of them. I did all I could to cover up my inappropriate sexual actions through my many community involvements. In the prison treatment program is where I began to look behind the masks I wore in society that allowed me not to recognize or acknowledge the harm I was doing through my sexual offending behavior and the attitudes that enabled it. Looking behind the mask is how I began to answer the question "Why?"

I also covered up a lot of anger that I wasn't aware of. It is another aspect of the sexual abuser/offender that few consider. In examining myself on this point, I had convinced myself that I was not angry with anyone. I didn't yell or scream or lash out at people, but those are not the only responses to anger as I later found out. After a lot of soul searching, I was able to come up with a list of about a dozen people that I was angry at in one way or another. Such anger did play a part in my sexual offending as I look back. Anger is often an excuse used for sexually abusing/offending someone. Sometimes it is the more subtle anger that can eat away at us. It has been said that anger, rather than a feeling, is a response to pain, shame, or fear. The sexual abuser/offender can experience one or all three—I claim at least two out of the three.

I didn't recognize the anger as such but knew I harbored negative feelings towards certain individuals. I fooled a lot of people—including myself—that I was "Mr. Nice Guy" who could do no wrong. But I, as with many sex abusers/offenders, know how to deceive others to get what we want. Sometimes, although we wear a "mask" trying to hide our negative selves, we need people to really see us for what we are, to cut through the deviousness, the false façade we put up, in order to bring us out in the open to help us. I needed help but did not know how to pursue it—and to pursue it meant trouble.

Keep in mind this important thought, "Sexual abuse is not about intelligence, race, class, or social status," [21] as it crosses all lines. It is about power and control; it is about individuals seeking to meet their perceived sexual needs/wants regardless of the feelings of others.

"Sexual abuse is a national health problem in America. Estimates vary, but the most common statistic cited is that one in five children may be sexually abused prior to age 18 and one in three women may be raped during her lifetime....these figures suggest a pattern of epidemic proportion."[21] Unfortunately, many sexual abuse situations go unreported or unproven. That has to stop! It is extremely important that as a nation we need to understand what constitutes sexual offending and what can be done to reduce the incidence of it.

"The only *rule* that should guide one's sexual decision-making and behavior is 'thou shalt not sexually manipulate, abuse, or take advantage of another at any time." [10] **(Emphasis added) It is about choice; and the ultimate goal should be to choose not to make any more victims of inappropriate sexual behavior.**

It is worth mentioning at this point that sex offenders in the prison system are regarded with disdain by other non-sex offender inmates, corrections officers, and staff. They are tolerated but usually do not respond to or treat them very well. Other inmates have many names for sex offenders: tree jumper, pervert, baby raper to name a few. It doesn't make any difference what level of sex offending was done. To them a sex offender is all of the above and more. I had to endure the taunts. I survived but it was not always easy going.

Chapter 3

Pre-Abuse

"Pre-Abuse consists of a series of behaviors, thoughts, and feelings that do not necessarily end up in criminal behavior but often set the stage for abuse to begin."
Anonymous

What is it? Pre-Abuse does not necessarily mean that offending behavior has been pre-planned, though that certainly could be part of it. Basically, it is **all the thoughts, feelings, and behaviors**—both short and long term—that had been going on within one's life prior to the offending behavior. It is a compilation of those three concepts, usually developed over time, but may also be of short duration. In my case, I had made a **choice** that inappropriate sex would be my deviation from society's norms. As time went by, my thoughts, feelings, and behaviors allowed me to **choose** to act out my sexual needs/wants/fantasies whenever I felt <u>opportunity</u> presented itself. I emphasize "choice" and "choose" because regardless of what I may think was driving me, I, in fact, made a choice between not abusing or offending, to abuse or offend.

Though age appropriate females had been my quarry in the past, young developing girls had held my interest for a long time. Being in close proximity to them merely heightened that interest allowing me to act against them when the opportunity came about. And I was able to create that opportunity at times. As for my family member living with us, I began seeing her as a surrogate wife and that allowed my mind to make the choice to sexually abuse her. Again, for my own benefit certainly not hers. Going through the SOP was a struggle! I had denied my sexual problems for so long that being forced look at them objectively was extremely difficult. That's why I had to finally break my life into somewhat measurable segments, as noted in Chapter 1, so I could more clearly see how I got to this point in my life.

As has been said before, sexual offending <u>does not just happen</u>. The following was taken from the June 29, 2004, <u>Our Daily Bread,</u> and lends credence to the "It Just Happened" fallacy.

"It's A Long Story"

"In August 1989, a major fire broke out under an elevated section of New Jersey's Interstate 78. The intense heat buckled parts of the highway and forced the closing of the east coast artery. The governor said it was the worst transportation crisis in years. An investigation brought to light a longstanding problem. It revealed that the fire broke out in a dump site in which construction debris had been collecting for many years. The owners of the site had been convicted of a multimillion dollar conspiracy to allow the illegal dumping of construction debris. But appeals in federal and state courts frustrated New Jersey's efforts to clean up the area. Not until the day after the fire did a state appeals court finally order the operator of the dump to stop accepting trash and begin clearing the site.

"That fire tells a basic story of life. **Most of our problems don't just happen. They are the result of a long series of bad decisions.**" (Emphasis added)

There is a method for understanding our behaviors (See A-B-C Model below) and "...is derived from the notion that one's emotions stem from one's beliefs, evaluations, interpretations, and reactions to life situations."[8]   Albert Ellis, who developed the model, maintained that it is a person's **belief** about an event, not necessarily the event itself, which drives his/her feelings and behaviors. One's belief about an event can be effected by one's mood: how one feels; and one's past experiences. Did something similar happen in the past and what was the response at that time? Our thoughts and feelings are often triggered (set off) by each other—a thought recalls an old feeling; a feeling can recall a past occurrence. You can have a series of escalating thoughts and feelings (feelings and thoughts) and behaviors before finally acting out on them. However, in the final analysis, behavior usually follows a thought then a feeling. Going back to Chapter 1, I can see how that played out in my life. Lack of proper sexual understanding and years of pornographic usage helped create my mindset regarding sex. Again, despite my education and my supposedly moral stance, I was able to throw all that away and act on what I felt was a basic need (or want)—sexual relief.

A-B-C Model

A = Activating Event: What started the thought pattern? I had to look back at my history to see how my thoughts developed that enabled me to act on an opportunity.

B = Belief   Your mood—good or bad
about event   Your past experiences—
                              pleasurable or not

Certainly one's mood plays a large part in how one reacts or acts to a particular event. A bad mood can be expressed as "I don't care; I want what I want." If past sexual experiences were pleasant for us, it is understandable that one would want to repeat them. If it was not pleasurable, it can go one of two ways:

1) Avoid similar events or,

2) Keep trying to find that elusive pleasure.

C = Consequent Behavior/Feelings: Results of acting/reacting upon Activating Event (ignore the event or act and wind up in trouble)

In short, what happens after the decision whether to act or not on one's feelings: prosecution or peace?

It is important to note again that we go through a variety of thoughts, feelings, and behaviors many times during a day. Some we are not necessarily aware of, that is why it is important to stop and take a look at our thoughts and feelings, and even our behaviors, several times a day to help us see possible negative trends. "Perceptions affect attitudes, which affect behavior."[9] "What you perceive [see] starts a chain of thoughts, feelings, and behaviors."[9] Being incarcerated gave me a lot of time to analyze my thoughts, feelings, and behaviors. I only wish I had taken the time before I offended to get in touch with them. Unfortunately, it is seldom something we do until forced to.

Our thoughts can also be influenced by what are referred to as "thinking errors." These "errors" distort reality and result in a person feeling bad about himself/herself or they may be used to protect oneself from bad feelings. We all have used one or more of them, often without realizing it. The more we use them, the more they become part of our life's pattern and shape our responses when faced with any possible life altering event. It has taken a while, but I do take a lot more time thinking before I make choices. Some notable thinking errors are:

Minimization: A person tells him/herself that something is not a big deal. The importance or impact of a situation is minimized or lessened [in their eyes].

Rationalization: A person makes up a reason or excuse to "explain away" a good or bad event/situation.

Overgeneralization: A person assumed that the good or bad result on one situation applies to all situations or areas of life.

All or Nothing Thinking: Things are either black or white, good or bad. Reflects a focus on extremes with no middle ground.

Denial: A person tells him/herself that a good/bad event never happened. Many people accomplish this by telling other people that the event did not happen, so they eventually believe it themselves.

Exaggeration: This is the opposite of minimization. Exaggerating usually blows a bad situation out of proportion, resulting in extreme negative feelings.

<u>Emphasizing the Negative/Minimizing the Positive</u>: Focusing on the negative aspects of a situation that has both positive and negative aspects resulting in negative feelings.

<u>Jumping to Conclusions</u>: Interpreting situations or other people's behavior without enough factual information.

<u>Personalizing</u>: Believing that others' behaviors or comments are directed towards you when they are not, or when you hold yourself responsible for something that was not under your control.

<u>Blaming Others</u>: Thinking that others are to blame for actions that you should clearly take responsibility for.

NOTE: Some of these terms will appear again in Chapter 9.

Sex offenders often have mistaken and damaging beliefs and attitudes regarding sexuality. Although, as I mentioned earlier, I am educated, I let pornography and peers' stories dictate my sexual standards. Such "stories" distorted my thinking process and affected my responses in certain social interaction situations. I found myself both listening to and communicating sexual stories and comments which can make others feel ill at ease and thought nothing of it. Demeaning sexuality is just another way to build up our inappropriate view of the sexes and allows us to act out without caring about the other person. It may seem contradictory but, "Each of us has a public self and a private self. The public self is the 'you' everybody knows. Hidden from view, however, is your private world—a world of fears, desires, dreams, and fantasies that you reveal only under certain conditions." [8] (The "masks" we wear.) If I, as a sex abuser/offender, do not change my course of thinking and monitor and understand my feelings, then the possibility of more sexual abusing/offending of others could occur. **I can't let that happen!**

Another way to take a look at ourselves is to see ourselves as made up of five parts[8]:

1. **SPIRITUAL SELF.** "Your spiritual self is not just about religion. It is about feeling whole and feeling connected to others and the world

around you. Your spiritual self plays an important part in meeting your need for belonging.

2. **EMOTIONAL SELF.** "Your emotional self directly affects what you think and what you do. All people have and experience emotions and feelings. As children, we begin with four basic emotions: **sadness, happiness, anger, and fear**.

Having and experiencing emotions is the key to leading a healthy life. Your emotions help you meet your need for mastery.

3. **PHYSICAL SELF.** "Your physical self includes both your physical being [your body], and what you do. Your physical self is directly linked to your need for independence. You develop your physical self through being responsible, being a leader, and taking care of your body and your health.

4. **MENTAL SELF.** "Your mental self is the motor behind everything you do. Your mental self is your thinking self and is critical for

meeting your needs for generosity. When you feel happy and content and your thinking is healthy, you enjoy giving to others, sharing, and making others feel good through your generosity. A healthy mental self gives you a sense of wholeness in your life. Your thinking affects your emotions and your behaviors. Everything you do requires either a conscious or subconscious thought process.

5. **SOCIAL SELF.** "Your social self is that part of you that people can see on day-to-day basis. In essence, it contains parts of the other four aspects. What is important, however, is how you and others see yourself as you interact with society. Are you standoffish? Do you mingle? Do you gravitate more to men, women, or children? Do you avoid people in general? It is these social interactions that people see and upon which they often make judgments." (In Reference 12, Bay and Longo include this part under the Emotional Self.)

Spiritually: Prior to my offending behaviors, I had accepted sex as my "sin of choice," even though I did have feelings of guilt, I felt okay with myself and my role in the community. However, after my arrest, I felt **morally** and **spiritually** bankrupt. I felt abandoned by my church and totally disconnected from the life I knew. How was I going to cope? I saw a bleak future ahead of me.

Emotionally: I had been emotionally stagnated for a long time. I held my feelings and emotions in check. I was concerned about me yet unable to express deep seated thoughts and feelings. I did not know how I was affecting other people nor did I seem to care. Depression had set in but I wasn't aware of it as such. I did not consider my busyness as a compensation for depression

Physically: I was in reasonable shape for my age. However, it was the fact of my age that bothered me. I wanted to think young, be young. Obviously, the latter affected my **mental** self.

Socially: As mentioned before, I was an active participant in many organizations so felt accepted. Such acceptance was not without feelings of insecurity. Knowing my mindset and my behaviors, I knew that I was going to be labeled a sex offender if I got caught. That alone would, and did, cut me off from all the things I had been involved in before getting arrested. I knew life was going to be different, but I didn't know just how different it was going to be. I was still in a state of denial of wrongdoing.

As noted, there are a number of factors that go into establishing a pre-abuse mentality. The primary way to prevent the buildup of such a mental state is to monitor the various factors that can affect your sexual attitude. Yes, there are a lot of things to consider. It would also be helpful to list the various factors so they can be conveniently referred to. The chart on the next page may serve as a day-to-day guide (may not be all inclusive).

<u>My Daily Mood Chart</u>

<u>Event</u>	<u>Yes</u>	<u>No</u>
Do I minimize negative things I do?	☐	☐
Do I make excuses?	☐	☐
Do I see events with a single viewpoint?	☐	☐
Do I make a big deal out of negative events?	☐	☐
Do I emphasize the negatives and not the positive events?	☐	☐
Do I "jump to conclusions" without all the facts?	☐	☐
Do I quickly blame others for negative events in my life?	☐	☐
Are my thoughts often on sexual matters?	☐	☐
Am I having sexual feelings?	☐	☐
Am I taking time out of my day to act out sexually?	☐	☐
Do I feel good spiritually?	☐	☐

Do I have negative emotions?   □   □

Is my physical health such that I do not need
to rely on others for help?   □   □

Am I in a good mental state — no negative
sexual thoughts?   □   □

Do I socialize with positive people?   □   □

Do I socialize with negative people?   □   □

Am I stressed out?   □   □

What is causing me to be stressed out?   List on back

What things make me angry?   List on back

Note: There may be many more that fit your emotional/psychological makeup; particularly when it comes to the stresses in your life. The last item "Anger," is an area that people often overlook but can have a devastating effect in regards to sexual offending/abuse.

Chapter 4

Grooming

"Grooming is the offender's plan to make the victims less likely to resist..."

Anonymous

Although the term "grooming" has a somewhat pleasant connotation, e.g., grooming an animal to make it look and perhaps feel better, when it comes to sexual abusing/offending, the word has a far more sinister meaning. To the potential sex abuser/offender, it means getting the intended victim to conform to what the abuser/offender wants to enable the offending behavior. **Remember, sexual offending is only for the benefit of the abuser/offender.** Consequently, doing such things as buying gifts, treating special, doing special things with the intended victim are all ways of getting an intended victim to conform to the abuser/offender's desires.

What can start out as seemingly innocent actions, can become sexual grooming when the grooming actions change from the "innocent" to the "intent" to do sexual harm. Once you set your mind on having sexual contact with someone, child or adult, you have established the

73

INTENT to abuse/offend. With intent in place, anything done for the intended victim to make it possible to gain access to him/her is called grooming. Grooming is done to break down barriers to enable the sexual abuser/offender to get closer to his/her victim. As the barriers come down, the intended victim develops a trust, a special relationship, with the abuser/offender. The groomer can do little wrong in the eyes of the intended victim so is often able to introduce "innocent" sexual content into other activities to further advance the intent to sexually abuse/offend. And, of course, the potential victim has no idea that grooming is taking place.

As noted again in Chapter 1, I was a member of many positive organizations. I joined them for all the right reasons—to be an active participant in the life of my community. Being so involved put the spotlight on me as someone who could be trusted—a good, positive role model. Consequently, no one would suspect me of harboring sexual offending tendencies—nor did I initially. However, once my intent changed and I started sexually abusing my two victims, all the "good, positive role model" stuff could be considered *grooming* in the eyes of the community once I got caught.

As one of my victims was a family member, buying her special gifts, giving her money, allowing her access to my computer, and letting her listen to music she wasn't supposed to listen to all seemed innocent enough at first, but became grooming when my intent to sexually abuse/offend her came into play. With my other victim, as she was a friend of the family member, I flattered her, tickled her, and joked with her. She was a recipient, through my family member, of special favors through the money I gave the family member. Once again my thoughts, feelings, and behaviors came into play in setting up my offending behavior. The whole idea of grooming is to subtly prepare an intended victim to be sexually abused.

Grooming involves not only the intended victim but also others as well. Building trust and breaking down barriers to gain access to the intended victim within the intended victim's family and/or circle of friends can also be considered grooming. There are three major types of grooming: physical, psychological, and grooming the social environment.

Physical Grooming

By definition, physical grooming involves physical contact with intended victims. It is such an easy "game" to play and attempts to desensitize potential victims to sexual contact. Adults, as well as children, like physical contact. Hugs and kisses are some of the ways we show true affection. The difference in physical contact between that which is intended to show affection and that which becomes a prelude to sexual abusing/offending is generally very subtle.

Again, I go back to a very important word—INTENT! When the physical affection begins to play with the mind of the giver of the affection, it can set in motion a chain of events that change the affection, perhaps innocently reciprocated, into a "he/she likes/loves me" attitude that can lead to escalated behaviors referred to in Chapter 1. That's how it worked for me. In other words, simple affection changes to offending behavior because the intent has changed. As used over and over again, the thoughts, feelings, and behaviors we develop over the years, create the atmosphere that allows sexual abusing/offending to happen when opportunity presents itself. Part of the grooming process can be setting up the opportunity by planning ways to get the intended victim alone or at least in a situation that allows the offending to occur.

Such escalating behaviors can include, but are not limited to: patting the buttocks, "accidental" touching the vaginal/penis area over clothes, the breast area, brushing the victims hand on the erect penis/vaginal area with the clothes on, to eventually exposing the penis/vagina and encouraging the victim to do the same. In the case of children, a lot of these behaviors can occur during ordinary play-- even in close proximity to other adults.

Of course, in the process of escalating the behaviors, the offender is also observing the reaction of the intended victim to determine the level of acceptance of the inappropriate behavior. If the offender senses reluctance from the intended victim, he/she may back off to a behavior that was more acceptable to the intended victim and possibly make a joke or simple excuse for the sexual contact. The offender then may proceed more slowly until he/she feels the intended victim is becoming more receptive to their touch.

Most of the foregoing grooming actions apply to children. When it comes to adult victims, although some of the elements of touching may apply, some offenders do not take "No" for an answer and use more direct actions such as: sharing pornographic materials of various types, buying drinks, drugging a drink, using or sharing drugs, getting a reluctant intended victim into a car or to another private place under some pretense. Presenting and enacting a fantasy scenario that has fascinated the offender may also be used to obtain the sexual gratification they feel they want or deserve. Over the years I used several of these methods with age appropriate women. You'll hear it again but **"No"** means **"No!"**

Psychological Grooming

Part and parcel with physical grooming is the grooming of the intended victim's mind—or psychological grooming. Not that an intended victim's mind is necessarily going to be convinced that what the offender is doing is acceptable or not, but rather that the offender is putting someone in a situation, both physically and mentally, to facilitate sexual abuse/offending.

The offender, during physical grooming, may tell the intended underage victim how special he/she is—that he/she even loves him/her. That what he/she is attempting to do is just a little step above the "playing" they have been doing and is okay. Perhaps trying to convince a child that what he/she is about to do is normally reserved for adults only but makes a point to give the victim a sense that he/she is really more grown up than the parents let on and is, therefore, entitled to learn about sexual matters. The victim is often told that he/she is very special to the offender and wouldn't do anything that will hurt him/her. If this is not the first time the offender has abused the individual, he/she may even say that this is the last time. I used that line myself. It is a promise seldom kept!

Also included in this category is the idea of bribery, intimidation, and threats. Exposure to pornographic material may also be used in an effort to convince a child that others are doing what the offender wants to do so it is okay. Young minds can be very impressionable. Too often someone whose <u>intent</u> is to sexually abuse someone, takes advantage of a child's innocence as one of their most useful tools. Anything that either puts the intended victim (adult or child) in a position of feeling obligated to the offender or in fear of harm to themselves or someone they love may also be used.

Bribes include many things but often involve the promise of money, gifts, or other things the intended victim may have expressed an interest in to be given either before or after sexual "favors." We've all heard the warning to kids, "Don't accept candy from strangers." Of course there is a lot of truth to that. However, it is a fact that most sexual abuse, whether on a child or an adult, is done by someone the victim knows. Intimidation can occur simply by the size of the offender in relation to the victim or the position the offender may have in the eyes of the victim; for example: a family member, teacher, church leader, or some other position of authority. When bribes and intimidation fail, the offender may resort to using threats. That if the intended victim does not comply, his/her parents or a friend might be hurt or even a pet injured or killed or the intended victim would be sent away (if a child). Also, if the offender is a family member, saying that if the offender was told on, it would cause the family financial problems and even to break up, can be a huge fear for a child—and a guilt trip as well if they do not do what the offender wants.

The abuser/offender is always thinking and looking for ways to achieve sexual contact once INTENT has been established. He/She manipulates people to achieve his/her ultimate goal. **And it is not about love! It is about power and control over another human being despite what the offender may say.**

Remember, a child under the legal age of consent (usually under 18) to sexual activity, or someone who is mentally or physically handicapped, **is never** the guilty party in sexual abuse despite the offender's claim that the victim "came on to me," or such other excuses. As for those of legal age and sound of mind and body, the guiding rule is mutual consent by both parties. Excuses that the victim was just playing around and really wanted sexual contact or that the victim liked rough sex are not valid. Neither is a claim by the offender that the victim was high on booze or drugs and did not resist sexual advances is also no excuse to sexually abuse/offend someone. They are just another "choice" to make the abuser/offender's behavior explainable in their own mind. That the intended victim was high on booze or drugs and did not resist sexual advances is also no excuse to sexually abuse/offend someone.

Psychological grooming is very damaging to the victim for it often raises doubts in their mind concerning what part they are supposed to play; how are they supposed to act? Was the abuse their fault? How will it affect them in future relationships, though not a concern at the time, become, along with many other problems, something the victim may have to deal with for quite some time with or without professional counseling. That the victim has been changed is not in doubt. More of both short and long term harms that a victim may experience can be found in Chapter 5.

Grooming the Social Environment

Simply put, to groom one's social environment is to put people at ease. The sexual abuser/offender often makes himself an important part of his community in a variety of ways so that when he/she is discovered, people find it difficult to believe that the person could have done what he/she did, or is alleged to have done. I know that was the case in my arrest. There is also the opposite—the loner, or that person who is frequently found in the company of those much younger. Or the person who seems to have trouble maintaining an age appropriate relationship, for example. One's involvement may, in its initial stages, be innocent. There is no doubt in my mind that I used all three of these grooming techniques in gaining access to my victims.

Again, even though the preceding text refers primarily to children, many of the same concepts applied to children are used on adult victims. Befriending someone, initiating "innocent" contact, e.g. brushing against, hugging, a kiss on the cheek, a dance, can be preludes to more forceful actions. Praising someone, encouraging them to follow a dream, plying them with drinks and/or drugs to weaken their resistance can all be construed as psychological grooming. For some sex offenders, taking someone out to dinner and/or entertainment constitutes a debt and thereby feels entitled to sex. Nothing could be further from the truth. **No one is entitled to sex. It must be mutually agreed upon by people of legal age, sound of mind and body, without**

any coercion whatsoever. And remember, "NO" means NO!

"In evaluating a relationship with another person to determine if it has the qualities of right relation, i.e., is grounded in love and justice, one might consider the following:

- Do I share the power equally in this relationship?
- Do I respect the wishes of the other person and my own regarding intimacy and physical or sexual contact?
- Do I trust that the other person will not betray or intentionally injure me?
- Do I freely and with full knowledge choose to interact with this person?
- Does the other person freely and with full knowledge choose to interact with me?

If these questions can be answered affirmatively, then persons can assume that the possibility of right relationship exists between them." [10]

There is one final element that needs to be considered—grooming of the abuser/offender. Obviously such grooming is done by the abuser/offender and can take such forms as a total disregard for the feelings of others, negative attitudes about women and/or children, and even "That's the way I was treated" attitude. Also, the acceptance of deviant sexual fantasies. Last and by no means least, is the offender's lack of care about self so that his/her consequences of getting caught in an inappropriate/illegal sexual activity has little to no impact on the decision to offend. I was warned several times about my seemingly suspicious behaviors and the consequences that could result if in fact I was doing something wrong. I ignored the warnings, I was in denial—I was that deep into my sexual addiction. The consequences tore apart my life and that of the victims, my family, the victim's families, friends, and associates.

Chapter 5

Your (My) Victim(s)

*"You **must** understand what your victims have experienced and are experiencing because of your crime."*

Robert E. Longo, et al

Who are my victim(s)? Obviously, they are the people I directly or indirectly (e.g., pornography) violated by using them for my own sexual gratification (though keep in mind, sexual gratification is not always what sexual offending is about). But that is only the tip of the iceberg. The "collateral damage," the extended victims, have been harmed as well ("harmed" does not have to refer to physical harm) and they can be extensive. Such extended victims are: my victims' families, friends, co-workers (if any) and my family, friends, and co-workers (if any). In the bigger picture, my community in general has been victimized. All of these extended victims suffer in various ways because of my actions as a sex abuser/offender. Love and trust issues have been affected. Community pride and security have been compromised. There are also both short and long-term effects on the victim(s) of sexual abuse/offending (and to some extent the extended victims as well).

One of the key terms used in defining sexual offending is *objectification* and was briefly described in Chapter 1. Simply stated, it means looking at a person as an *object* of sexual desire with no regard for the person's own thoughts, feelings, or welfare.

"Not only is this sexual objectification unhealthy <u>for both addicts and non-addicts</u>, it is also addictive for sex addicts. This is so because anytime a sex addict **thinks** of another human being as a sex object, that addict's addiction is engaged and inviting a destructive outcome over which they have limited control."[18] "What is acceptable for others can destroy us." [18]   [Emphasis added]

It is the "I want what I want when I want it" thought of the sexual abuser/offender regardless of what the other person may want. Many experts in the field are clear that sexual assault and rape are more about power and control than about sexual gratification. "Being raped [in the eyes of the victim] is like getting a life sentence for a crime [they] didn't commit.[12]"

There are three primary factors that are useful in differentiating abusive from non-abusive acts—Power, Knowledge, and Gratification Differentials. These three factors are often interrelated. The presence of any one of these factors, when considering a sexual encounter (legal or illegal), should be cause for concern.

Power Differential

Just using the term "power" is enough to envision a person much bigger or stronger than the victim. Although that may be the case, particularly with children, that is only part of it. Strength is not the only power weapon that can be used. As mentioned in Chapter 4, power can come from the position of the offender in relation to the victim. Teachers, group leaders, church leaders, family members (particularly parents) all wield a lot of power (authority) over an individual. Using such position, it is much easier to manipulate intended victims into sexual contact by using promises of better grades, promotions and such—or threats of harm to victim or others.

Knowledge Differential

Often a person's knowledge can be used to sexually abuse someone. Again, this can be used with younger victims where the more worldly knowledge of an abuser/offender can impress and confuse a young mind. It can also be used against those less educated or someone mentally challenged regardless of their age.

Gratification Differential

Who benefits from sexual abuse? Obviously, not the victim! Although an abuser/offender often attempts to justify his/her actions by convincing themselves that the victim was getting sexual satisfaction. Even the abuser/offender does not always achieve sexual satisfaction. All too often what the abuser/offender realizes is not sex but the momentary thrill of being able to have power and control over someone. The abuser/offender may also gain satisfaction through the successful planning and carrying out of the offending behavior.

There is no doubt in my mind that, as with the grooming types in the previous chapter, I used all three of these differentials in my sexual offending of my two

91

victims. However, gratification was the primary purpose for my sexual activity regardless of whom I was with and power was the primary "tool." Admittedly, my ego often convinced me that the victim would enjoy it too. And keep in mind that when someone is sexually assaulted/abused, it is considered <u>forced</u> sexual behavior. Again, it does not necessarily mean physical force, but simply the fact that a sex act was done against another person without their permission or they were not of legal age or of sound mind and/or body to give such permission. If you don't think what you did was aggressive, I suggest you reread the three "differentials" mentioned above (power, knowledge, and gratification). Then take a good hard look at what you did (or plan to do or would like to do to someone).

There is something called the "Continuum of Sexual Aggression" which runs the gamut from viewing individuals as sex objects to sexual homicide. I don't think I need to be graphic about the latter. Once a person is thought of as a sex object, the offender can envision him/herself considering all manner of sexual activity (deviancy) that his/her sexual wants/fantasies can conjure up. Again, we can go back to the "escalating sequence of behaviors" mentioned in Chapter 1 to see how "innocent" sexual activity can escalate into sexual offending where an innocent person is violated.

How do you measure up as an abuser/offender/re-offender or potential offender? There have been a variety of offender typing studies done. However, there is considerable disagreement among professionals on whether such "typing" is valid. Though for me, in reviewing the various "types," I had no problem identifying with the Regressed Type and the Incestuous Father Type and felt they were a reasonable tool for me to use in self-identification. For the "Regressed Type," although my primary sexual interest was age appropriate women, I became fascinated and excited by developing young girls. In short, I regressed to my early pubescent years to seek sexual satisfaction. Due to that fascination, I placed myself in the "Incestuous Father" category and used my "father figure" persona to carry out my sexual offending against a family member and her friend.

There are so many aspects of the "whys" of sexual offending it could take a book of its own to describe them all. Suffice it to say, if one spends an inordinate amount of time, as pointed out earlier, thinking, feeling, and behaving in a sexual manner, it may become a problem that can lead to, or may have already led to, sexual abusing/offending. Recognizing that, it is time to consider seeking professional counseling or other similar help to reform one's pattern of sexual thought and conduct. Being in prison was a good example as to how one's actions affect another person. Corrections Officers make no bones about their feelings towards inmates, especially sex abusers/offenders. Their treatment of such inmates should give a good idea how victims may feel (e.g., belittled, emotionally hurt, and thought less of)

For myself, if I had to define one item that had the biggest impact on my sexual thought processes, it would have to be pornography as noted in Chapter 1. It is everywhere and can be defined from the very public ("soft") sexual displays on TV and in movies to the blatantly hard core pornography as shown in XXX rated movies, books, magazines, and, especially in these times, the internet. "Through many of the [pornography] industry's products and services, consumers can be victimized through the alteration of their perceptions about human sexuality, by acquiring distorted views of human sexuality…"[21] I can certainly claim that viewpoint for myself. Unfortunately, it is such a controversial subject that "To address this issue is to step into a morass of controversy that raises questions about the meaning of sexuality and the nature of pornography, its effects on human behavior and the question of censorship."[21] As I noted in Chapter 1, I took from pornography two thoughts, 1) women wanted and enjoyed sex and 2) women were to sexually please men. Both very wrong interpretations! Enough exposure to such material can effect the production of the powerful internal drugs mentioned by Dr. Carnes in Chapter 1. Sexual fantasies can develop and build to a desire for reality—whether that "reality" is with a willing partner or not. Again, being in touch with your thoughts, feelings, and behaviors can go a long way in understanding and, hopefully, curbing one's excessive sexual desires.

Sexual abusing/offending is also about values. As mentioned in Chapter 1, I subscribed to a number of positive values through the organizations in which I was involved. However, I let my wants, or perceived needs, and sexual misinformation/misunderstanding overshadow those values. I consciously made a choice to throw away all my values—I became INTENT on sexually abusing my family member. Developing a sense of empathy (to be covered in Chapter 8) through the in-prison program helped me put those positive values back in the forefront of my thoughts and feelings.

To commit any crime is a **CHOICE! It is a choice I made**. I can't blame my upbringing—neither can anyone else. No one put a gun to my head to commit rape or any other so called "crime of passion." I *chose* to violate another human being because I lacked empathy; I lacked caring for the feelings of others. What governs your sexual choices when making a decision in regards to having sexual contact with someone? It has been said that not making a choice is, in fact, a choice. When it comes to sexual offending, it is a choice that will cause harm to an innocent person. See the last page of this chapter for a more comprehensive list of problems victims may face.

As for my primary victims, both required extensive psychological counseling. One made a suicide attempt.

One of my extended victims also made such an attempt. Although both attempts were done long after the offending behavior stopped, I take a good share of the responsibility for their actions for my actions impacted on their lives. Though I was no longer part of their immediate lives, had I been there for them, had I not sexually offended, perhaps the attempts would not have occurred. I also had a significant impact on other extended victims—especially to my immediate family, but many friends suffered as well by the loss of trust as well as other issues that occurred.

One important point that must be made perfectly clear regarding the concept of being a victim—those who commit sexual offenses **are not** victims. Okay, maybe they were abused as youth and are, therefore, a victim of those events. Maybe they had a lousy childhood and are a victim of poor parenting. Perhaps they felt they were a victim of the "system." None of the foregoing, or any similar event, is a valid reason or excuse for sexual abusing/offending! If anything, we are a victim of the bad choices WE freely made. We may be a victim of thinking about WHAT WE WANT and not caring about others. Perhaps we are a victim of OUR OWN self-made thoughts, feelings, and behaviors. We may also be a victim of the pain, shame, and fear that resides within us. That is called ANGER. And we attempt to get rid of that anger by lashing out at others—AND THAT IS WRONG any way you look at it

Common Problems of the Sexually Abused[21]

"Victims of sexual abuse react differently at some levels and very much the same at others. Below is a partial list of some of the more common problems seen in children who have been harmed by sexual abuse:

fear of specific persons	fear of specific places
advanced sexual knowledge	fear of the dark
anxiety	withdrawn behavior
fear of males or females	fear of harm to family pet
alcohol/drug use & abuse	anger
depression	self-mutilation
loss of appetite	excessive appetite
nightmares	runaway behavior
poor school performance	flashbacks
behavioral problems	sexual promiscuity
sleep disturbances	aggressive behavior

insecurity

behavior regressing
to an earlier age

sexual acting out
(inappropriate sexual behavior)

fear of being alone

compulsive behaviors
(e.g. excessive bathing)

fear of abandonment

fear of something happening to a
close friend or family member

irritability

"Adult victims of rape and sexual abuse may show many

of the above plus some additional ones such as:

sleep disturbances

eating disorders

somaticized emotional pain

fear of specific persons

fear of specific places

anger

fear of being alone

fear of being out of the
home (agoraphobia)

fear of males or females

depression

feelings of inadequacy

anxiety

insecurity

loss of control

suicide ideation

low self-esteem

compulsive behaviors

withdrawal

sexual dysfunctions

denial

marital/relationship problems   sexual addiction

"Neither of these lists is exhaustive, and certainly persons experiencing other traumas can have similar symptoms, but they are representative of the more common problems faced by sexual abuse victims."

Chapter 6

Learned Behavior

"Being abandoned through the neglect of our developmental dependency needs is the major factor in becoming and adult child. We grow up; we look like adults. We walk and talk like adults, but beneath the surface is a little child who feels empty and needy, a child whose needs are insatiable because he has a child's needs in an adult body. This insatiable child is the core of all compulsive/addictive behavior."

John Bradshaw

So, how do we learn about sex and all that that subject entails? To some extent sex education is taught in schools; it should be taught at home. Unfortunately, it is far too often learned from our peers (who are just as misinformed as we are), inappropriate materials (soft and hard core pornography from a variety of media presentations), and from experiences that may also have been inappropriate. My learned behavior can be summed up as a combination of most of the above. In the words of Gail Ryan and Sandy Lane, "Sexual abusers are not born abusive."[17]

"The things we are exposed to have a profound effect on the way we think and view things in general. These thoughts manifest themselves in the way we carry ourselves and act, i.e., our behavior. This process is known as *Learned Behavior.* We act or react to the events in our lives based upon our experiences; be they positive or negative."[8]

We start learning from Day One! We learn from family, friends, pastors, teachers, and other such community leaders—and these learning experiences can be both positive and negative. We soak up all this information, but if we don't have someone to guide us through the maze of sometimes conflicting sexual messages, we can become a candidate for sexual abuser/offender status. As mentioned several times, I subscribed to the moral codes of many fine organizations yet succumbed to the lure of pornography early on which impacted my sense of morality and subsequent behavior. I declared myself to be "sexually amoral" (if it felt good, do it) resulting in my various sexual encounters and eventual sexual offenses. I made a choice and convinced myself that most of what I did in life was good. One "small sin" would be outweighed by the good I did. How wrong I was!

It is essential to look back and see how our sexual "code of conduct" developed. Becoming aware of our inappropriate sexual behaviors, recognizing where they may have come from (maybe not specifically), and helps in developing a more positive approach to such behaviors. As noted in Chapter 1, it took prison to teach me that positive sexual conduct involves much more than just the physical element—there are spiritual, emotional, psychological, and ethical dimensions as well. I doubt that sex ed or parental teaching covers all of that. So that was quite an eye opener for me! It is also important to note that becoming aware of our sexual shortcomings is not an excuse for acting out inappropriately towards another person. Bryan Robbins, in his book, *Heal Your Self-Esteem*, sums up the answer to learned behaviors by having us tell ourselves "...I cannot control everything that happens to me, but I can always take charge of what I will think, feel and do under every circumstance."[22] [Emphasis added.] In other words, we can stay trapped in our old ways or reach out and embrace a new way of thinking, feeling, and behaving.

I feel it is important to consider the various developmental stages we pass through: infancy, pre-school, school age, adolescence, and young adult. In each of these steps we are introduced to a variety of life's lessons where the "seeds" of our sexual functionality are planted, nurtured, and developed. <u>Warning:</u> Even if the "seeds" are discovered, <u>they do not justify sexual abusing/offending on our part!</u> I know in Chapter 1 I explain finding my "seeds" of sexual disinformation and it may appear that I used them to justify what I did. On the contrary, it was to point out the foolishness of that notion. I was educated. I knew right from wrong—but chose to do the wrong thing for my own personal gratification.

In the young adult stage, we find that "Boys get messages that [we] are supposed to act a certain way in order to become a 'real' man."[8] We are often taught to hide our emotions ("Don't cry."), to be fearless and in control. They are referred to as gender (or sex role) messages—that as males (or females) we are expected to act a certain way.

In considering the above, it is so important that a proper and wholesome approach towards sex be established at an early age by parents and reinforced as youth go through the initial stages of their lives. Without the right sexual attitude, youth seek answers in less accurate and proper ways thus creating the chance that misinformation can later lead to inappropriate sexual behavior. I can certainly attest to that! Dr. Carol Ford, an associate professor at the University of North Carolina School of Medicine, in an article published in the Sunday (Schenectady, NY) Gazette, March 12, 2006, entitled "Parents likely affect adolescents' attitude towards sex more than they know," taken from a study published by the Archives of Pediatrics and Adolescent Medicine, cited that "...the findings indicate that parents should make their view on sex clear to their children." In our modern society, fraught with sexual innuendo around us all the time, and the magnitude and high number of sex crimes, it would appear that parents are falling short on that duty. We as adults, and perhaps parents, may use pornography and be comfortable watching sexually intense programs/movies, yet we can't seem to convey to our children proper sexual ethics. Was it done for me? No! And did I do it for my own children—NO!

Another aspect to sexually learned behaviors is the idea of keeping secrets and shame. There is a saying that goes something like this, "We are only as 'sick' as the secrets we keep." (I believe this is an AA maxim.) What are these secrets? Many of them are of our own making due to our sexual actions that we can't talk about for fear of being labeled a pervert or being arrested. They are also those things we have been taught in the family that we aren't supposed to talk about: e.g., grandpa's drinking, Uncle Joe's womanizing, and the like, that help make our view of the world a somewhat secret place. It is easy to become less caring about the feelings of others when we are burdened by our own personal load. As with others, I just wanted to free myself from the pain and shame I felt over my actions despite the way I thought about myself (sexually amoral).

"Secrecy provides a way to hide criminal acts and also plays a part in violence and sexual aggression. When pain from experiencing bad things feels unmanageable, some people get confused and try to cover up the pain with anger. Desperate and confused needs for power and control and connection, mixed up with secrecy, can influence misdirected anger that results in violence and sexual aggression."[16]

As for shame, perhaps we have been belittled by family and/or peers, not to just ourselves, but often in front of others. We develop an attitude that says we are worthless and therefore don't care about what we do or who we do it to. Secrets and shame eat at us. If left unchallenged, they can begin to define who and what we are. They can lead us and our future relationships into a dysfunctional state that has an impact on how we think, feel, and act—not just sexually but in other ways as well. "Often a shame based person is not aware of his negative self-image because of his false self-cover up. We become so identified with our Role or Script, we are no longer aware of our deepest feelings about our self."[6] Most shame weakens us and makes us targets for those who want to dump their negative self-image on someone else. I learned that the hard way in prison. However, recognizing what is shaming us can be a catalyst for positive change—a way to rebuild our own self-images.

Yes, I did indeed suffer shame. I knew what I was doing was wrong but felt powerless to stop. Though I tried, my efforts were unsuccessful. Who could I talk to about my actions? No one that wouldn't get me in trouble! Instead, I attempted to deal with my improper behavior knowing full well that if I got caught it would be devastating to my family and others—it certainly was! Such shame was eating at me at about the same rate as my inappropriate acting out. It was a vicious circle! I felt bad about what I did; I thought I needed to relax; I felt stressed. How did I relax? By either masturbating or abusing and in both cases received the pseudo-calming effect of ejaculation (often referred to as the 60 second high)—then back to shame.

It can be said of sexual offenders, but particularly sex addicts,

"In fact, addicts can't love themselves. They are an object of scorn to themselves. This deep internalized shame gives rise to distorted thinking. The distorted thinking can be reduced to the belief that I'll be okay if I drink, eat, have sex, get more money, work harder, etc. The shame turns one into what Kellogg has termed a '**human doing**,' rather than a '**human being**'." [6]

[Emphasis added]

NOTE: Before reviewing the next segment which looks at the progression of sexual offending, and shows how learned behaviors can play out, it is essential to reintroduce the concept of sexual addiction mentioned in Chapter 1. It is also necessary to again clarify that all sex offenders are not sex addicts; but it is safer to say that sex addicts are more likely to become sexual offenders. In a presentation before a class of drug addicts, inmate Thomas Draughn made the following statement: "....addiction takes over often when people fail to provide the immediate 'feel good' remedy a person needs. The person will then replace people with 'objects' that give them that fast satisfaction they need—drink, drugs, sex [where people become objects for the purpose of satisfaction]." I feel it is important to add that when you feel you NEED sex to relax or get a hold on your life, it is not unlike NEEDING a drink or NEEDING a drug fix. It is the way your body (and mind) are telling you something else is controlling you rather than yourself. That "NEED" then becomes a "WANT" and unless you can recognize the warning signs, you may begin to do whatever it takes to make that connection.

The following also refers to the "escalating series of behaviors" previously mentioned and are, therefore, relevant to those whose sexual habits/desires may be getting more physical and mental play than they should.

Three Levels of Sexual Addiction

There are three defined levels of sexual addiction. Each level alludes to the general thoughts, feelings, and behaviors going on within a potential sex addict. As one goes from the lowest to the highest level, it shows how an addiction can develop. **One does not set out to become an addict of any kind,** but the pattern of one's thoughts, feelings, and behaviors pave the way. And those three elements are usually a product of the potential addict's own family and life experiences—in short, *learned behaviors*. "To interrupt the addictive cycle, the addict must understand his own unique pattern of behavior and creating a framework for the behavior will make that task easier."[8] (See Chapter 9 regarding identifying one's Sexual Offending Cycle.) Think about each of these Levels and ask yourself, "How does this relate to my thoughts, feelings, and behaviors?"

Level One: The simplest form of sexual gratification is probably masturbation. It is a natural and private occurrence but is often labeled as inappropriate behavior by parents and some elements of society. Consequently, using it as a release of sexual tension, can also produce feelings of guilt and may develop a feeling of confusion and degradation. "It feels good but I'm told it's bad for me."

However, as the feeling of pleasure becomes the driving force, it often becomes necessary to feed the mind with fantasies which aid in completing the gratification. That may lead to consuming pornography and other sexually explicit material to increase sexual stimulation. Though the behavior may be stopped for varying time periods, it seldom goes completely away. "The problem with Level One addicts is that they can rationalize that they are no different from other folks. Yet the addict pays a personal toll in increasing pain and loneliness."[8]

Level Two: This level shows how the escalating sequence of behaviors, mentioned earlier, comes into play. The potential addict can generally deal with Level One activities for just so long. When those activities become commonplace and the level of satisfaction drops, it often becomes necessary for the addict to find a new level of sexual excitement. Exhibitionism and Voyeurism are generally the next logical escalating steps where the potential addict gets bolder. I tried both of those in my youth, and to some degree in my later years.

As an **exhibitionist**, the potential addict may use as simple an approach as leaving his zipper open to actually exposing himself (flashing) in public (or secluded areas where the chance of getting recognized or caught is diminished). Some have even been so bold to try streaking. And, of course, as the level of inappropriate activity grows, so does the level of anxiety—"What if I get caught; the humiliation!" Without counseling the activity rarely stops and can heighten the excitement of the event.

Voyeurism (also known as Peeping Tom) has a "simple" side too, such as visiting porno shops, theaters, and strip clubs. The more advanced Level Two addict goes to the extreme and looks for windows to look into either directly or by telescope. Of course, if the potential addict succeeds in his exhibitionistic/voyeuristic activities, his excitement builds leading the way to move on to Level Three activities. Though there are laws forbidding both of these Level 2 practices, they are considered more of a nuisance than a threat or actual harm. They may not be seen by the general public or the law enforcement community as escalating sequences of behavior yet often lead to more serious sexual activity.

Level Three: With the start of Level Two, personal boundaries of others are being violated. The victim may not know they are being victimized for they have every reason to believe they are safe walking down the street or being within their own home. With Level Three activities, the victimization becomes up close and personal. Rape (Again, having sex with an underage person, adult sex without mutual consent, or sex with someone who is not mentally or physically capable of given consent is all covered under rape), incest, and child molestation become the next level of sexual acting for the potential addict.

Real people are now replacing the fantasies induced by Level One and Two activities.

Each of these levels develops at the pace the potential addict feels he can deal with. And, of course, does not necessarily realize or understand the progression of these events and where they can lead. Moving from one level to the other may only take days for some and weeks, months, and years for others. When I first read about the three levels, I easily saw my progression of behavior—my addictive behavior. Unfortunately, it was too late for me for I had already sexually offended. May it not be too late for you.

There are many psychological aspects attached to these levels as well—from Level One and the fixation of self-generated sexual gratification and the various feelings evoked by that activity, to the escalated self feelings of the other two levels. But with Levels Two and Three, there are the personal impacts the sexual activities have on the victims and extended victims. Such impacts cannot be minimized—they are extensive!

It is essential that the potential addict, or for lack of a better way to put it, the sexually frustrated/ compulsive person, needs to recognize his/her actions and the direction in which they are leading him/her. To do so it will be necessary to spend a lot of time on Chapter 9 in recognizing and developing a Sexual Offending Cycle. Although it is called a Sexual Offending Cycle, it can be used by someone who has not yet offended by pointing out one's thoughts, feelings, and behaviors that could lead them to the point of offending. By identifying them, a non-offender may see problem areas to work on or may recognize that professional help may be needed before they act out. The attached chart provides a comprehensive explanation of the above.

In summary, we all learn about sex in some manner. How we use that information can make a difference in the enjoyment we get out of life and the relationships we have along the way. A wholesome, positive view of the sexual part of our lives is important to that end.

Of course, there is a whole range[17] of adolescent and adult sexual behaviors that can be classified as anywhere from normal   to extremely provocative. Under "normal" might be such things as "playing doctor;" "you show me yours and I'll show you mine;" and sexual jokes to name a few.   Others, such as pornographic usage, promiscuity, touching, peeping tom, exposing oneself, and boldly getting someone into a sexual situation that could have serious life consequences.

LEVELS OF ADDICTION[4]

LEVEL OF ADDICTION	LEVEL ONE	LEVEL TWO	LEVEL THREE
BEHAVIOR	Masturbation, hetero-sexual relationships, pornography, and homosexuality	Exhibition-ism, voyeurism, indecent phone calls, and indecent liberties	Child molestation, incest, and rape
CULTURAL STANDARDS	Depending on behavior, activities are seen as acceptable or tolerable. Some specific behaviors such as prostitution and homo-sexuality are sources of controversy.	None of these behaviors is acceptable.	Each behavior represents a profound violation of cultural boundaries.
LEGAL CONSE-QUENCES/ RISKS	Sanctions against those behaviors. When illegal, are ineffectively and randomly enforced. Low priority for enforcement officials generates minimal risk for the addict.	Behaviors are regarded as nuisance offenses. Risk is involved since offenders, when observed, are actively prosecuted	Extreme legal consequences create high-risk situations for the addict.

VICTIM	These behaviors, are perceived as victimless crimes. However, victimization and exploitation are often components.	There is always a victim.	There is always a victim.
PUBLIC OPINION OF ADDICTION	Public attitudes are characterized by ambivalence or dislike. For some behaviors such as prostitution there is a competing negative hero image of glamorous decadence.	Addict is perceived as pathetic and sick but harmless. Often these behaviors are the objects of jokes which dismiss the pain of the addict.	Public becomes outraged. Perpetrators are seen by many as sub-human and beyond help.

From: <u>Out of the Shadows: Understanding Sexual Addiction</u>, by Patrick Carnes, PhD. Copyright by Hazelden Foundation. Reprinted by permission of Hazelden Foundation, Center City, MN

Chapter 7

Empathy

"Sex offenders are thought to suffer deficits in their capacity to experience empathy…"

W. L. Marshall, et al

What is empathy? Simply stated and using an old cliché, it is "Like walking a mile in another person's shoes;" or perhaps the more modern expression, "Been there; done that." It is the experiencing of something that when you meet someone in a similar situation, you have a feel for what they may be going through.

For myself, I know I have heard the word, and the above expressions, but somehow managed to allow myself to ignore them. As I found out during the Sex Offender Program, it is a term sadly lacking in the sex abuser/offender's vocabulary. "Sex offenders are thought to suffer from deficits in their capacity to experience empathy, and this is considered to be important in the development and particularly the maintenance, of their deviant behavior."[20] Remember, sex abusing/offending is all about the person abusing/offending. The feelings of others involved are not considered.

Most of us have experienced some painful event in our life—and I don't mean just physical pain but emotional pain as well, especially with the loss of a loved one. Perhaps we have been called names, told we were bad, stupid, careless, or many other such labels. Sometimes we were told something enough we began to believe it. We remember how bad we felt. If a friend lost a child but I have not, I can sympathize (feel sorry for) but not necessarily be able to show empathy. However, if I lost someone extremely close, I can have a sense of what the other person is experiencing. That is empathy. If I can look at the intended victim as someone's sister/brother, daughter/son, for example, and how I would feel if someone violated my family member, I can develop a sense of what my victim, or intended victim, might go through—that, too, is empathy. If you can relate the pain you felt to how you were treated, to how the victim will or may be feeling, then you are experiencing empathy.

There is no way we can ever feel or understand exactly how another person has been affected by sexual

125

abuse. Each person deals with a traumatic event in their own way. Enough studies have been done to show that the damage is extensive and can, in come cases, last a lifetime. Many of the short and long term effects were shown in Chapter 5. We may try to forget the hurts done to us in the past, but it is seldom totally successful and can often effect how we respond to other events in our lives. As said before, one thing must be perfectly clear, **any abuse done to us is never an excuse to abuse someone else.**

I remember others in the program I attended who were appalled at what someone else had done and what they would have done to them if they had done it to a member of their family. At the same time, they minimized (See Defense Mechanisms in next chapter) what they had done to someone else. I can even remember my acting outraged at sexual offending articles in the paper yet failed to see my own actions in the same light. When a first cousin of mine got arrested for child sexual abuse, my wife said I went ballistic. Again, not recognizing my own actions! Far too often we look at abuse or violating ones rights in terms of physical harm, as mentioned earlier, causing pain, leaving bruises, or, in the extreme, causing death. Not doing any of these things, we convince ourselves that we didn't hurt anyone. How wrong that is! Therapy may lessen the impact, but the event will always be a part of life.

Developing Empathy

Developing empathy is essential in helping prevent sexual abuse/offending. "Learning to feel empathy doesn't 'happen' overnight: you have to develop it by practicing over and over; just as you have to do pushups over and over to develop your muscles."[14] There is some controversy over how much empathy plays in the role of a sex offender, but it appears that most of those who have studied the subject agree that a lack of empathy is a significant component of the sex abuser/offender makeup. Therefore, it is an important concept to consider. "The development of victim empathy facilitates [eases] the healing process and makes it more difficult for the sex addict [abuser/offender] to return to his old behaviors by:[11]

> (1) Reducing denial regarding the impact of sexual behaviors on self and others.

(2) Taking ownership of the behaviors and 'facing the shadow.'

(3) Experiencing appropriate guilt and shame.

(4) Eliminating objectification and compartmentalization.

(5) Beginning the process of integration with the hope and goal of developing integrity."

"There are four poisons[12] that kill empathy: urges, anger, twisted thinking, and denial." Giving in to any one of these "poisons" can result in sexual abuse/offending.

Urges: "An *urge* is a powerful desire to get something you want, immediately, regardless of how or at whose expense...Urges go beyond basic wants or needs."[12]

It becomes a driving force; an unquenchable thirst for satisfaction. We often say we have the "urge" to kill or punch somebody out. Fortunately, we seldom act on such urges. However, when we feel the urge to satisfy our sexual wants, we throw empathy out the window (if we ever had any to begin with) and "...begin to look for and manipulate potential victims."[12] We don't care, or rather don't think, about another's feelings in the matter. We want what we want whether we really feel satisfied or not in the end.

Anger: We all get angry from time to time. It is quite normal and natural. Anger can be as subtle as expressing ourselves in a sarcastic manner to being violent where we lash out physically at the person or persons making us angry; or at anyone else that may get in our way. Obviously, the person you land on would feel equally bad—and you just might run into someone who does not practice empathy (or anger management techniques) and a very stressful situation for both could result. What often happens is we let our feelings and emotions build up while trying to act as though nothing is wrong. Then, seemingly out of the blue, we explode. It was just one more "little" thing, the proverbial "straw," that finally overwhelmed us and we let loose. This buildup of unaddressed feelings is poisonous! (Remember, anger is considered a response to fear, pain, or shame or a combination of those three.)

"When you use empathy, you break the cycle of anger. It's like putting brakes on a wheel that is spinning out of control."[12] To express empathy means that you have taken the time to gain control of yourself and realize that there are at least two sides to an anger situation. There are a number of studies on anger and the problems it can cause when expressed inappropriately. Anger management is a required program for incarcerated sex offenders (in New York State at least) because much of sexual abusing/offending can be linked to anger issues. One can take many positive steps in attempting to curb inappropriate sexual behaviors, but if anger is not addressed, most other positive steps taken may fall victim to the unresolved anger issues.

Twisted Thinking: In Chapter 3 it mentioned Albert Ellis's Rational Emotive Therapy for understanding our behaviors. Two key elements of that therapy are critical to the poison that is "twisted thinking:" one's **mood** and one's **experiences**. We are all subject to mood swings; we can't be happy all the time. Some days we are just in a bad mood. We got up late, didn't sleep well, troubles, illness and the like affect how we feel—and, unfortunately, how we often act. An event that on any other day might have been taken in stride can be cause to blow up based on proven or unproven thoughts and feelings. "He did that on purpose." "They have been out to get me for a long time." Perhaps a similar negative situation occurred in our past and we see the current situation in the same light and act accordingly. A reliance on mood and past <u>negative</u> experiences to determine our current behavior is a recipe for disaster and goes against being able to show empathy.

Denial: This will be covered in more detail in Chapter 8. However, knowing you did something wrong and denying it is a failure to accept responsibility for one's actions regardless of what brought about those actions.

So, how can you develop something you don't understand? "Most men and women who have no empathy have shut off their own feelings of fear, shame, pain [components of anger], confidence and joy..."[11] They react to situations they find themselves in by using defense mechanisms (See Chapter 8). "When you shut off painful feelings, you also lose the ability to experience positive feelings."[11]

That is why I put so much emphasis on getting in touch with and understanding your thoughts, feelings, and

131

behaviors. Until you can understand them and express them in a positive manner, you cannot begin to understand the thoughts and feelings of others—which, in my opinion, is the heart and soul of empathy.

We all have feelings whether we wish to acknowledge them or not. So long as we hide those feelings from ourselves, we also hide them from others who may truly wish to know the "real" or "whole" you. Not being able to understand how we feel, makes it difficult for us to have positive relationships and happiness. We allow those hidden feelings to place a dark cloud over our lives which can cause negative thinking and even explosive behavior. I had to really dig into my past and open long closed doors to my feelings to see how I lacked empathy and how I negatively expressed my feelings. It was not an easy process—but certainly a necessary one. No matter how intensely painful, or sorrowful, or depressed you are about what you may have done as an abuser/offender, your victims felt and feel worse. "Keep in mind, that the focus of empathy is not how **you** feel--it is how **others** feel."[11] (Emphasis added.) You don't have to give up power in your own life to feel empathy—trying to put yourself in the victim's place is actually a show of strength. You become able to show caring and restraint in what may be a difficult situation. Instead of acting out in anger or self-interest, you are able to show that you do care and do have feelings for others. Disgust about what you may have done is an appropriate and realistic feeling. Being disgusted with yourself for the pain you have caused and the people you have hurt is a step in the right direction. But it works only when you can use this feeling to motivate yourself to change. If you are not committed to change, being disgusted with yourself is another form of self-pity and it only feeds your abuse cycle. (See Chapter 9). The key to developing empathy is learning to think and feel **before** you act.

Another way to prevent or reduce unpleasant situations is to share your negative thoughts and feelings with someone else—a spouse, co-worker, boss, counselor, 12-Step sponsor, etc. They, in turn, may be able to help put the negative feelings to rest before a confrontational situation occurs. Hopefully, the person with whom you share your negative thoughts and feelings, will be one who is able to respond with empathy (been there; done that) and be, therefore, able to "walk in your shoes" for a moment. As with any skill, as previously noted, empathy must be practiced over and over again. Consequently, you must have regular interaction with people in order to develop the skills necessary to be able to practice empathy.

I can say now that empathy is part of my vocabulary. I have seen the hurt, confusion, and anger that my actions have caused. I would not like to be the cause of bringing those feelings to anyone else. It is important, again, to constantly monitor my thoughts and feelings in order to ensure that my behaviors are appropriate.

One of the strongest learning aids regarding empathy used in the treatment program that I attended was listening to an actual 911 tape of a rape in progress. It was heartrending! A poem written by one of the inmates after hearing the tape best captures the mood of the moment:

<u>The Pain, The Pain, Who Felt The Pain I Feel?</u>

Who felt the pain when you wept silently?

The pain of helplessness?

The pain of anguish?

The pain of agony?

The pain of hopelessness?

The pain of dejection?

The pain of loneliness?

The pain of fear?

The pain of shame?

The pain of loss?

The pain of horrors?

The pain of terror?

The pain of sadness?

Who felt your pain

When you cried for help

And got none?

Who felt your pain

When you screamed?

Who felt your pain

135

When hopelessness and helplessness

Caused you to regress?

Who felt your pain

When you lost the confidence

Of being an adult

And whimper as a helpless child?

Who felt your pain?

Oh! If only

I had felt your pain

Before I caused it?

Perchance it would have

Stopped

Me from harming you.

Your pain enlightened my thoughts

And touched my chromosomes "X"

The part I was taught

To make tough

Not to feel, speak or trust!

So I could lock my pains away

Behind the flood-gates

Of feeling

Manhood of objectivity

Allowing me to objectify

So I wouldn't

Know how to empathize.

Twisting my mind

In agony

While I stuffed my feelings

Of humanity.

I've felt your pain

And it brought me

Back to reality

So I've decided

To give up my cognitive sexual deviancy

So I can rise above

My primal state of brutality.

Yes, I've felt the pain of your reality!

Errol Irving   October 13, 2004

Chapter 8
Responsibility/Defense Mechanisms

"New life requires both forgiveness and confession. For offenders to be truly whole, they must confess wrongdoing, admitting their responsibility and acknowledging the harm done."
                                                            Howard Zehr

"Responsibility: I did it…" Perhaps the most difficult part of coming to grips with committing a sexual crime, or doing anything wrong for that matter, is taking responsibility for it. And that comes in the form of "three little words"—"I did it!" But it goes much deeper than that.

When it comes to sexual abuse/offending, it isn't enough to just say, "I did it." It is necessary to acknowledge and accept full responsibility for all of the various acts done to the victim(s) as well as all of the different harms to the victim(s) both during the offense and its aftermath. Remember, there are also "extended victims" as well that have been harmed and it is necessary to acknowledge one's responsibility towards them also.

140

"For the offender to think otherwise is for him to assign partial or full blame to others. Such is not the case! As the offender, you are totally responsible."[8] It makes no difference whether you feel the victim came on to you, or you feel he/she wanted sex as much as you did, if the victim said no, struggled, was underage, mentally or physically impaired, you are in the wrong if you pursue your sexual **wants**. Accepting responsibility and all the ramifications of what was done, is a necessary step towards being able to understand and develop empathy which we covered in the previous chapter. It is also important to consider "road blocks" to accepting responsibility for our actions—and they are referred to as *Defense Mechanisms.*

Defense Mechanisms

From all indications it would appear that we are nearly perfect individuals. When something goes wrong or something bad happens to us, we are quick to pass the blame on to someone or something else. We are not at fault. As sexual abusers/offenders, we often blame our parents, the way we were raised, lack of education, pornography, past sexual abuses upon ourselves, or the alleged victim "came on to me" and other such excuses. I was a blamer too! **There are no valid excuses for sexually abusing/offending anyone!**

What are defense mechanisms? They "…are psychological tools people use in order to avoid dealing with thoughts or feelings [or behaviors] that cause them pain." [8] People use defense mechanisms in an attempt to avoid all types of discomfort and incriminating situations (illegal activities, e.g.). "People who become defensive are unable to recognize: 1) that they have problems, and 2) how seriously those problems affect their lives. The more they use defense mechanisms, the harder it is for them to accept that they need help."[8]

How do you recognize that defense mechanisms are being used? First you need to recognize what they are. Here is a list of some of the more common defense mechanisms:

a. **Denial:** In short, we don't like to be wrong so we make up every conceivable excuse to deny that we did anything wrong.

We:

Don't

Even

k**N**ow

It's

A

Lie!

b. **Rationalizing:** We try to make sense of what we did by trying, as an example, to make a comparison between what we did and actions by others that we claim to be similar to ours. Ex: What he did is far worse than what I did."

c. **Justification:** We claim the actions were deserved because of some previous action by someone else. Ex: "She hit me first."

d. **Religiosity:** Claiming "all of a sudden" you got religion and that will take care of past and future mistakes in judgment.

e. **Intellectualizing:** Attempting to cite various facts, figures, and research to add credence to one's actions.

143

f. **Blame:** As already noted, we are quick to blame others or things for the actions we take.

g. **Projection:** We are also quick to point out the flaws in others in an attempt to lessen the severity of our own actions. It is a person's tendency to see and criticize their own faults that they see in others and at the same time not see them in themselves. [Boy, did I use this one!]

h. **Minimizing:** Trying to make what was done sound less harmful than it was.

Recognizing whether you are using *defense mechanisms,* now that you see some of the terms that apply, should be an easy process. However, if you have been lying to yourself for some time as I had done, lies have a tendency to take on a life of their own and can appear as the truth to the denier.

Since denial is usually the first of the many defense mechanisms used, it is important to recognize that there are different types of denial and levels of denial.

First and foremost there is the <u>complete denial of responsibility</u>. We flatly deny that we have done anything wrong. When that denial doesn't work, we usually claim we didn't have the <u>intent</u> to do anything; it was not <u>premeditated</u>—"It just happened." (Where have we heard those words before?) And of course, we didn't <u>harm</u> anyone in the process of whatever it is we are supposed to have done.

The <u>frequency</u> of the alleged inappropriate action(s) has, in our opinion, been greatly exaggerated—as has the degree of personal <u>intrusiveness.</u> (It wasn't that bad!) There are several other types but perhaps you get the picture. Whatever we do or say to claim something didn't happen or, if it did, we didn't do it or to the degree that is claimed, is some form of denial. **And yes, I used several of the defense mechanisms in my quest to be blameless.** As well as there are a variety of denial types, there are different levels of denial.

There are four levels of denial. They range from "weak avoidance" offenders: Those that basically admit their guilt; to "primitive denial/severe avoidance." The latter being the offender who flatly denies any involvement in offending behavior whatsoever.

Within the four levels of denial are a combined total of twelve types. These range from "minimal denial," or the simple admission of guilt without minimizing or justifying; to the person who gets extremely "hostile, delusional, or defensive."[8] I don't feel it is necessary to go into the specifics of each level or type. Suffice it to say, it appears to be human nature to deny wrong doing. When challenged we can act passively or aggressively depending on our mood, past experiences, and level of anger within. Obviously, the higher the level of denial coincides with the higher the type.

Now that there is (or should be) an understanding of defense mechanisms, how they work, and why we use them, it is necessary to examine ways to overcome them. "Why would I want to do that? My denials just might work!" Yeah, right! In denying a wrong doing, it is only prolonging the inevitable—the truth and the consequences thereof.

I recognize telling the truth seems like a coward's way out. I denied any wrong doing when challenged by family members. I had convinced myself I could get away with my sexual abusing/offending. However, once confronted by the truth through the admission by the abused/offended persons, I could no longer hide from it.

Since sexual abuse/offending has already harmed a number of people, denying one's part in the abuse/offending only continues the harm and can add additional persons to the list. We abusers/offenders know we did wrong. We must face up to it. It is not an easy thing to do but it is not the end of the world for us— though indeed, our world will change. We can take our lumps like an adult and then work to rebuild our lives— and perhaps the trust of others. No, it is not easy to admit guilt. But it is necessary if we are ever going to regain a sense of balance and purpose in our lives. It is time to act responsibly!

Chapter 9

Sexual Offending Cycle

"In fact a cycle is like a rotating circle. A cycle refers to a pattern that repeats over and over."

Robert E. Longo & Lauren Bays

From a letter written by a child abuser:

> "Early in my treatment my therapist said to me, 'Your task in therapy is to change your entire style of being alive.' I was stunned. I didn't understand what she meant. I felt frightened, overwhelmed by the enormity of it. 'I'm a sex offender,' I thought. 'I'm in jail because I need to change my deviant sexual behavior. Why is she dragging in the rest of my life?'

> "As I progressed in treatment, I came to understand what she meant. My deviant and destructive cycles are not separated from the rest of my life."[9]

So, what is the "cycle" that is talked about? Simply stated, it is the routine of one's life. It is the thoughts, feelings, and behaviors that progress through a series of definable steps that, unless interrupted, may lead to sexual abuse/offending—or any other inappropriate behavior for that matter. Identifying one's cycle is to help "…understand that behavior does not occur spontaneously. Rather, any behavior is the product of a complex interaction between thoughts, feelings, and behaviors"[8] in order to recognize negative trends and correct them before inappropriate behaviors occur. It is essential to understand this interaction and be able to apply it to one's own life.

Sexual offending behavior, as with other negative behaviors, usually goes in cycles. There is a definitive pattern that can be isolated and identified. Much of life runs in cycles be it work or pleasure (we often refer to it as ups and downs but it is more complicated than that). The following scenario is a good example of how thoughts, feelings, and behaviors work to create a cycle.

In the reporting of a basketball game, a reporter, along with the rest of the crowd, was astounded by a shot one of the players made that won the game. When the reporter asked the player how he made such a shot, the player's comment was "The ball was in my hands, the situation was right, so it **just happened.**"

Did it just happen? Years of playing and practicing made it possible. The player's <u>thoughts</u> were on the game, he <u>felt</u> prepared, and his <u>behavior,</u> because of all the practice, made him ready when <u>opportunity</u> presented itself. And that is often the way it is with sexual offending. Whatever I did over the years to create a negative sexual mindset and the <u>feelings</u> that mindset generated, made offending <u>behavior</u> possible when <u>opportunity</u> presented itself. However, the grooming techniques discussed in Chapter 4 are the preparatory steps we take that make us ready when either opportunity or a specific plan to abuse/offend comes into play.

As I was in my 60's, I had to go back some fifty years plus and create my cycle. I did it in three distinct twenty year increments so I could see how my sexual dysfunction developed and what made up my cycle. It was a soul-searching process to say the least. If I don't watch my thoughts and allow them to wander into forbidden territory, my feelings could begin to build to the point that old behaviors may beckon. When opportunity presents itself, I could be ready to act out.

> "Your deviant cycle could take a few minutes to run through or it might take months. Once you let it start, you have two choices:
>
> - You can give up control [of your life] and let it take its course, as you have in the past.
>
>   [-OR-]
>
> - You can take charge and stop it.
>
>   The choice is entirely up to **YOU**."[15]

When developing your cycle, if you have already abused/offended, it is easier to work backwards from the abusing/offending behavior and try to identify those factors that led up to the behavior. If you have not yet abused/offended, you can still prepare your cycle by following the guidelines presented. It is also necessary to discuss the cycle with close family members, friends, and perhaps a trained therapist. Each of whom may see important points we may have missed. We don't always see all of our faults. The chart and accompanying definitions can usually point out the thoughts, feelings, and behaviors that led to the abusing/offending behavior. One help is to try and identify your habits—those things you consistently do. "Habits are well established chains of behavior that are strongly linked to your daily life."[9] Identifying these habits will help in recognizing negative ones that may impact on your cycle.

"There are at least nine[9] good reasons for you to study your [life cycles], especially your deviant cycle.

1. You learn what led up to committing your crime. The path from health to deviance is not simple.

2. By studying your cycle you learn that each of your actions has several causes and several effects. When you understand your cycle, you will learn about the causes (the behaviors, thoughts, feelings, and circumstances) that led to your deviant behaviors.

3. You learn how you usually react to thoughts, feelings, and environments.

4. You learn that your behavior is affected by every place you go and everything you see.

5. By studying your cycle you learn how your feelings influence your behavior.

6. You learn how your thoughts influence your behavior. Even in what appears to be an impulsive, spontaneous crime, thoughts set the stage for the behavior.

7. You learn how your beliefs about the world and yourself influence how you act.

8. Understanding your cycle teaches you how what you do today influences what you do tomorrow and in the future.

9. Understanding your cycle will teach you when and how to stop your deviant behavior. Knowing when to intervene is one result of understanding your deviant cycle." [9]

Unless you understand the repeating pattern or cycle of sexual abuse/offending, accept full responsibility for abusive choices, and **actively** learn and practice new, non-abusive habits and behaviors, you are at risk for continuing to abuse yourself or others. "Insights are helpful but without a sincere commitment to institute changes based on those understandings, danger remains." [21]

As mentioned in previous chapters, it is necessary for me to be in touch with my thoughts and feelings several times a day so I can recognize when my mind is drifting into negative territory. And I need to have a way to deal with those negative thoughts and that will be covered in the next chapter (Relapse Prevention).

Consider the cycle format that follows and the terms that apply. They should help you in identifying your own cycle.

1. Sexual Offending Cycle
2. Cycle Terms
3. Predisposing (Early) Risk Factors
4. Precipitating (Immediate) Risk Factors
5. Perpetuating (Ongoing) Risk Factors

1. SEXUAL OFFENDING CYCLE[8]

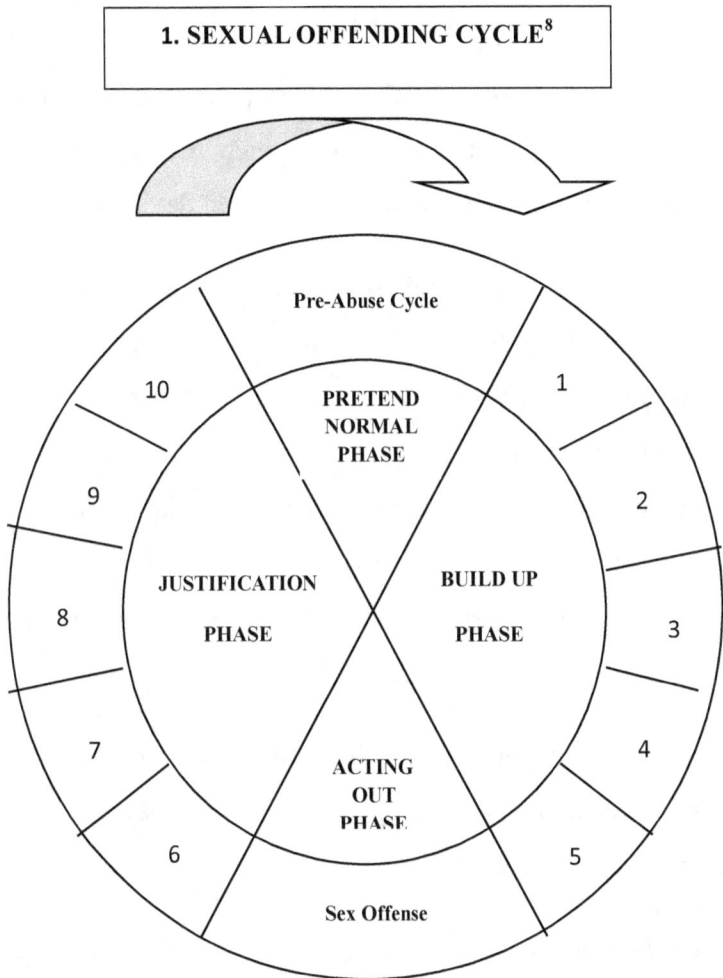

Pre-Abuse Cycle

PRETEND
NORMAL
PHASE

10
1

9
2

JUSTIFICATION
PHASE

BUILD UP
PHASE

8
3

7
4

ACTING
OUT
PHASE

6
5

Sex Offense

NOTE: See corresponding numbers for descriptions on following pages. This sexual abuse cycle represents an "average" offender's cycle and its various phases. The particular parts and their order within each phase may vary among offenders and some offenders may not experience all parts shown.

2. Cycle Terms[8]

Offending (Deviant) Cycle: The pattern of specific thoughts, feelings, and behaviors which lead up to and immediately follow the acting out of sexual deviance.

Pre-Abuse Cycle/Pretend Normal Phase: Consists of a series of small behaviors, thoughts, and feelings that do not necessarily end up in criminal behaviors but often set the stage of the above cycle to begin. [It is a transitional cycle in that it is the period where you have allowed yourself to "forget" about what happened and get back to some "normalcy" before sliding back into inappropriate thoughts, feelings, and behaviors.]

Perception: Is what you see, hear, feel, taste, or smell. In order to recognize something you must become aware of it, you must perceive it.

Triggers (Perceptions): "Triggers are behaviors, rituals, conditions, and people who in some way activate the addictive patterns. Some triggers are obvious, for example, calling or seeing old lovers even without being physically sexual. [It is how we perceive something and how it can recall thoughts, feelings, and behaviors that can "trigger" (start) sexual thoughts and perhaps lead to "mind games" thus drawing one into opening an offending cycle of behavior.] This is not unlike the drug addict who decides to keep a stash but not use it. Cruising old haunts is another obvious trigger."

"Some triggers are more indirect. Being depleted or emotionally overwhelmed leads to feelings of entitlement, which in turn provoke the addictive response. Some triggers are difficult to acknowledge, for example, being around family members who are shaming or abusive. [Acting out, in fact, can be a reenactment of the old family abuse patterns.]" (Patrick Carnes, PhD)

Links: Each segment in the chart is like a link in a chain. They connect one part of the chain with another. They are simple, often appear insignificant, and yet are vital. They are generally of two types:

> **Behavioral Link:** A behavior that naturally follows another behavior and leads to the next behavior.

Connector Links: Are the thoughts and/or feelings that always occur before and after a behavioral link.

Chain: A series of thoughts, feelings, and behaviors that follow one after another.

Build-up Phase: This is the part of the cycle where such things as planning, grooming, and deviant fantasies occur.

(1) Seemingly Unimportant Decisions (SUDs): Decisions which on the surface appear to have no relation to sex offending at all, but which an offender may know deep down inside will lead to high risk situations. They can evoke feelings of fears and powerlessness over sexual situations.

SUD's taken by themselves appear unrelated to offending when in reality each choice leads the offender closer to the point where he must make a final decision to offend/re-offend or not to offend/re-offend. They are decisions that at first seem to have little bearing on whether a lapse or relapse will occur. An example of a SUD would be:

- A pedophile who decides to go Christmas shopping at a mall on a Saturday afternoon is making a SUD. (In reality, the guaranteed presence of children in the mall allows the abuser to place himself in a high risk situation where he may lapse or relapse.)

Other examples of SUDs would be:

- Going to work late
- Not going to counseling
- Not paying bills
- Going to congested areas—schools, parks, etc.

(2) High Risk Factors (HRFs): Internal motivations or external situations or events that threaten your sense of self-control and increase your risk of lapse or relapse. High Risk Factors usually follow seemingly unimportant decisions and tend to draw us into situations that can lead to claim we are not responsible for our actions.

A high risk situation is an occasion that could immediately lead to an offense. Circumstances that threaten an individual's sense of self-control and increases risk of relapse. Some examples would be:

- A rapist who, driving his vehicle to escape an angry interaction with his wife, spots a female hitchhiker.
- A pedophile who is asked to baby-sit for a neighbor.

A high risk factor is any person, place, thought, feeling, behavior, or memory that could make you more likely to re-offend.

Encountering a risk factor does not mean that you will re-offend again. It is only a warning sign that you may start sliding into deviant behavior or placing yourself in high risk situations. If an offender manages to cope with a high risk situation, his sense of self-management survives. As long as his expectation of his ability to handle future high risk situations remains realistic, his probability of relapse decreases.

If an offender fails to respond adaptively to a high risk situation (for example, he purchases pornography while in a book store), his sense of self-management decreases and a tendency to passively yield to temptation in the next high risk situation may happen. Although some offenders lapse in situations which would have been difficult to anticipate, the majority seem to set the scene for relapse by placing themselves in high risk situations. This can be done unknowingly through a series of Seemingly Unimportant Decisions, each one which represents another step toward a tempting, high risk situation. When faced with HRF's, it is important to learn the escape and avoidance techniques covered in Chapter 10.

There are three types of High Risk Factors[8]: Predisposing (Early) Risk Factors, Precipitating (Immediate) Risk Factors, and Perpetuating (Ongoing) Risk Factors. (See the end of this chapter for a more definitive breakdown.)

(2 Continued) Maladaptive Coping Response (MCR): An effort to deal with a risk factor or lapse that enables you to get closer to relapse. An MCR allows you to move from the frying pan into the fire. To say it a different way, MCR's are an inappropriate way to cope with a difficult situation. For example, an alcoholic taking a drink because he is stressed out. Some other examples might be:

- An angry rapist decides to take a drive to cool off, and then picks up a female hitchhiker.
- A child molester decides to "relax" with a drink when he is upset, even though he knows drinking alcohol is part of his offense pattern.

(3) Lapses: [A lapse is a return to attitudes, thoughts, feelings and behaviors that lead back to the addictive or compulsive acts.] They are emotions, fantasies, thoughts, anxieties, or behaviors that are part of your cycle and relapse pattern. Lapses are not [necessarily] sex offenses. They are *precursors* or risk factors for sex offenses. Lapses are not failures and can be valuable learning experiences. [Remember, breaking old habits is difficult so a slip backwards is always a possibility.]

(4) Abstinence Violation Effect (AVE): This determines whether or not a lapse becomes a relapse. It is the many changes in your thoughts, beliefs, and behaviors when you lapse. When you experience AVE, you may mistakenly conclude that you have no willpower or are unable to change. You may think of yourself as a failure destined to always fail and want to give up completely. It describes how you feel when you've broken your promise to give something up.

You are most likely to experience AVE if you believe that you will never lapse. But when you are prepared to deal with the AVE, your chances of re-offending are decreased. You might also experience the **Problem of Immediate Gratification (PIG)** phenomenon. It is the individual's selective recall of positive aspects of having engaged in a deviant sexual behavior in the past. It occurs when you remember only the positive sensations experienced before, during, or immediately after committing a sex offense. By recalling only immediate positive sensations from past assaults, you increase the likelihood that you will commit another offense. You are likely to forget the negative consequences that are usually delayed, such as:

- Guilt   Shame
- Loss of family   Loss of friends
- Loss of employment   Jail
- Parole, etc.   Publicity about your
                            arrest and conviction

When you learn to counter the strength of the PIG phenomenon by focusing on the delayed negative effects of your actions and both the immediate and delayed harmful impacts on victims, you decrease your likelihood of relapse.

(5) Continued Lapses & MCRs: [See above for initial definitions.] This is the final phase before acting out. It is the last chance to recognize the impending negative sexual behavior and intervene to stop it. It is in this phase that Ryan and Lane[17] identify "The Decision to Act [or not to act]."

> "The decision to act occurs immediately prior to the sexual abuse behavior and appears to involve several factors: excitement, sexual arousal, thrill, risk, super-optimism, anticipation, empowerment, eradication of remaining inhibitions, and entitlement. Many youth [and adults] prefer to view their offense behavior as having 'just happened' and initially deny that they made an active decision to cross the line and sexually abuse someone." [17]

In short, it is where the setting up of the offense takes place and all the factors that go into the planning—fantasies, grooming.

Acting Out Phase: The actual commission of a deviant sexual act. The transforming of deviant fantasies into deviant behavior. After acting out, there is a moment called the **Waking-Up Stage:** It is what happens immediately after you commit a sexual crime. In order to perform deviant sexual behavior, you probably had to get into some sort of altered state of consciousness. You tend to become numb to your feelings and less aware of reality during the build-up phase of the cycle. But after ejaculating or completing a sexual act, you probably felt as though your mind suddenly cleared and you 'woke up' to discover what you were doing.

Justification Phase: "Justifications are rationalizations and distorted perceptions developed to support the youth's [or adults] sexual abuse behavior. The distortions help the … offender to overcome or erode internal prohibitions against the behavior and make the offense behavior seem reasonable. The perceptions are not temporary; they are enduring beliefs that are difficult to correct.[17]"

(6) Despair: Here such things as fear and guilt occur, and we start to use defense mechanisms (described in Chapter 8) to deny the problem; vows to "never do it again," but often does. Feelings of shame also are present.

(7) Defenses: It is usually normal to deny our wrongdoings so we do all in our power to stave off our guiltiness. We rationalize, minimize, deny, justify, and blame others. Again, these are defined in more detail in Chapter 8.

(8) Cover-up/False Remorse: Self pity rears its ugly head in this stage. Like defenses we try to hide our guilt and, to ourselves at least, tell ourselves we are sorry for what we did.

(9) False Resolve: This is simply a promise to ourselves that we will never do this again. Sometimes we say this to our victim(s) as well. It is a promise rarely kept. I know I used this one several times.

(10) Suppression: We try to forget what happened. Unfortunately it is part of us and, as the old adage goes, "If you forget the past, you are bound to repeat it."

Pretend-Normal Phase: When you finally have recovered enough physically and psychologically to be able to sense that your life is back on track, you feel almost normal, but due to (10) above, the cycle is ready to start all over again.

Although not a part of the cycle, the following terms can help you understand your thought processes and perhaps curb your deviant sexual behavior:

Thought Stopping: First, identify the thoughts you need to stop—your sexually deviant or violent fantasies, for example. You must be specific and clear about exactly which thoughts you want to stop. It won't work to say you want to stop "deviant thoughts," unless you first recognize them as deviant.

Sexual Arousal Conditioning: Learning to change your sexual arousal requires working with an experienced therapist who is skilled in conditioning techniques and the use of the penile plethysmograph. The plethysmograph is an objective way to measure sexual arousal.

Covert Sensitization: This is a sophisticated form of sexual arousal conditioning. The purpose is to replace deviant but pleasurable excitement with images of realistic and unpleasant consequences.

Fool Factor: The unexpected events that may throw you into stress and initiate the deviant cycle. These may be things such as putting yourself in places with people and/or things that activate your triggering.

Sexual Deviancy: A pattern of being aroused by inappropriate sexual stimuli in which there is a high probability of behaving in a sexually assaultive manner.

Grooming: The offender's plan to make the victim less likely to resist, to make others unaware of what he is doing, or even to make them likely to help him, without their knowledge; can be physical, psychological or can also be grooming of the social environment or the community. These were covered in more detail in Chapter 4.

Polarizing: Thoughts focus on seeing the world as two clearly different sides. What you think about is either right or wrong with no gray area in between.

Blaming: Pushing your responsibility off on someone else; not being accountable for your acts. One of the things we seem to jump to immediately after being confronted with an offense and is part of the discussion in Chapter 8.

Precursors: A general term used to describe what happens before you commit a sex offense, including SUDs, MCRs, risk factors, lapses, and the AVE.

> **NOTE:** It is important to mention that all the steps in the Build-Up Phase of the cycle provide an opportunity to recognize the backsliding and stop and regain control of yourself. Once you "cross the line" into the Acting Out Phase, you have offended/reoffended.

3. Predisposing (Early) Risk Factors[8]

These are events that appear to establish the foundation for your sexual offending behavior. They tend to happen during the childhood and adolescent years of the offender or they occur very early during the build-up toward sexual abuse. They are not—and never can be considered— excuses for committing sexual offenses.

Alcoholism in the Family	Cognitive problems/ learning deficit
Emotional abuse as a child	
Lack of Assertiveness	Limited education
Family chaos	Parental marital discord
Lack of sexual knowledge	Paternal absence/neglect
Maternal absence/neglect	Parental divorce
Sexual abuse as a child	Physical abuse as a child
Exposure to violent death of a human or animal	

4. Precipitating (Immediate) Risk Factors[8]

These are events that appear to stimulate sexual acting out and generally occur within the six month period prior to the offense:

Anger	Low self-esteem
Anxiety	Low victim empathy
Abusive sexual fantasies	Opportunity
Boredom	Over-controlled emotions
Cognitive distortions	Peer pressure
Compulsive behaviors	Personal loss
Cruising/aimless wandering	
Dependency on another	Physical illness
Planning a sexual offense	Depression
Pornography use	Disordered sexual arousal
Sexual anxiety	Divorce/breakup of relationship
Social anxiety	Isolation & Stress
Emotionally closed	Social skills deficit
Substance use/abuse	Use of prostitutes

5. Perpetuating (Ongoing) Risk Factors[8]

These are generally ongoing problems in your life and often help you in your cycle or relapse process:

Anger	Frequenting high risk situations
Abusive sexual fantasies	High risk employment
Boredom	Living near places where children congregate
Denial of problem	
Low self-esteem	
Drug/alcohol abuse	Marital problems
Dysfunctional intimate relationships	Masturbation to abusive fantasies
Frequenting high risk behavior	Use of pornography/ prostitutes

Chapter 10

Relapse Prevention

"We can 'mentally imprison' ourselves by clinging to our old ways of thinking, feeling, behaving or we can try new approaches to life."

Bryan Robinson

Another "mathematical formula" comes to mind: **Knowledge + Tools + Desire = Relapse Prevention.**

- Knowledge: Knowing yourself and why you abused/offended.

- Tools: Anger management, meditation, counseling, medication, e.g.,

- Desire: You can have all the knowledge and tools available at your disposal, but if you do not have the desire to change your thoughts, feelings, and behaviors, then *Relapse Prevention* probably is not going to happen.

Unlike a lapse mentioned in the cycle, which may be a singular incident of returning to one's old ways and then recognizing it, a relapse means that someone has again "crossed the line" and committed an actual offense.

The purpose of Relapse Prevention should be obvious. It is a plan to help the sexual abuser/offender, or the potential one, not do a sexual offense. As noted at the beginning of this chapter, there are three things necessary to help one keep from sexual abusing/offending anyone. It is not enough to say we won't do it. When asked if I could reoffend, my response was a qualified "Yes." If I allowed myself to recreate the same circumstances that existed when I abused and offended my two victims, it would not be impossible for me to reoffend. Therefore, I needed a plan to make sure it didn't happen. As part of my prison sex offender program, I had to create a realistic Relapse Prevention Plan that encompassed a number of factors that can help in my desire to "have no more victims." The "formula" above is, of course, a simplification of a longer program. Relapse Prevention takes time and is not something we can do entirely alone as will be explained later.

Consider life as a triangle with three equal sides representing the mind, body, and spirit. The three sides can also represent our selves, our family, and others. The three equal sides represent a balance. If too much effort is put on any one side, then the other sides suffer and the triangle becomes out of balance--life becomes out of balance. My life became out of balance. I allowed my mind and body to dictate my sexual expressions. My spirit, that part of me that should have put up warning flags to my behavior, was ignored. As for the second triangle, life was about me and my many associations leaving my family to physically and emotionally fend for themselves. When life's balance gets misaligned, it is easy to become frustrated, angry, stressed—all things that can aid in falling back into old habits that can lead to offending/reoffending. It can also be a sign of depression, an all too common ailment that can get overlooked. Men overlook it more than women—I know I certainly did.

As has been noted in previous chapters, sexual offenses do not "just happen." All we have to do is take a good hard look at our cycle and see how we prepared ourselves to abuse/offend. Sure it was not necessarily our original life's plan, but all the things we spent time on that were sexual in nature was leading us in that direction. We now have to "unwind" our negative sexual thoughts, feelings, and behaviors and find a way to keep them in check. That is why we need to prepare a detailed Relapse Prevention Plan (RPP).

> "The relapse prevention model suggests that there are no CURES for sexual deviancy. That is, no matter how strongly you feel that you will not commit another sex crime, if you make the wrong choices and allow yourself to indulge in distorted thinking, feeling, and action, your sexual problems will return. However, it is possible to live a crime-free life by following the steps of the relapse prevention model. … Every sexual offender has the potential to re-offend." [7]

An awareness of ones deviant cycle, which I covered in the previous chapter, is essential to preparing an effective Relapse Prevention Plan. If I am serious about "having no more victims," I have to be honest with myself and that can be hard to do—especially since I had been lying to myself for a long time (denial). When I finally got into the prison sex offender program, I learned things I had never really thought about before. As with the writer of the letter at the beginning of Chapter 9, I realized I needed to rethink not just my sexual attitude but my whole life attitude as well. I knew from the start that it wasn't going to be easy.

Relapse Prevention is a process. Just as developing negative habits did not occur overnight, neither will a RPP. It takes a lot of thought and effort to develop. If it is your sincere desire to create no more victims, it is a process well worth the effort.

Of course, the first step in developing a Relapse Prevention Plan is to acknowledge that a problem exists. And if you did a detailed cycle, you know that it does. If that declaration is not made, it will be impossible to prepare an effective plan because you will be prone to overlook certain thoughts, feelings, and behaviors as not contributing to the problem. You never know what may be the initiating "trigger" to an abusing/offending behavior so it is necessary to put down anything you can think of that consumes your time in any way. It is a whole lot easier to later remove a habit or behavior than to discover one that set you off too late. It will help to look back at the cycle and make two columns, for example:

Problem Area	Replacement (This goes into your RPP)
Pornography	Positive self-help books

Relapse Prevention goes through various stages. The process can be a benefit by making us look at our life as a series of pluses and minuses. Pluses are those things that are positive in our lives be they family, friends, job, hobbies, health, as examples. Minuses may be some of the same items but it is also necessary to take a look at other people, places, things, and our attitude that seem to emphasize our vulnerabilities and make it possible for us to backslide in a false effort to gain what we believed would make us feel better—sexual relief.

No discussion of RP can be complete without considering how to avoid the temptation to offend or re-offend. Two words are critical in this discussion: **avoidance** and **escape**. "**Avoidance** works on a simple principle; if you avoid people, places, things, situations, or events that are **triggers** [See "Cycle Terms" in Chapter 9] in your offense [/behavior], you will not reoffend."[14] (Emphasis added.) Although the principle sounds easy, avoiding all those "triggers" may not always be possible. "Once you have a trigger, you will always have a trigger.

Making avoidance a lifetime habit will help you not to reoffend."[14]

Unless we move to an entirely new area and completely avoid the types of people, etc. that may have contributed to our offending behavior, we are bound to run into them again: things (pornography, e.g.), situations (crowds, e.g.), individuals, or events (parties, e.g.) that also may have contributed to our offending. That is where **escape** comes in. If it is impossible to ensure avoiding risk situations, when faced with them, we need to have a plan to get away—if not physically, at least mentally, by developing "negative or positive mind games and/or self-talk" techniques to change our focus: think of going to prison (or again), embarrassment of family, and the use of non-sexual pleasant thoughts are just a few of the things one can do to divert their attention away from the triggering situation. "Thought-stopping has four steps.[14]

(1) awareness of thought,

(2) identifying undesirable thoughts,

(3) stopping undesirable thoughts, and

(4) replacing undesirable thoughts with healthy thoughts."

Then "you must do three things to stop deviant behavior and keep it stopped.

> (1) Admit the possibility of re-offending [It is wrong to think it won't happen again. If you do not understand deep down why and how your abusing/offending occurred, how can you tell if you are on the wrong path again?];
>
> (2) Plan how to stop the behavior at the earliest stages of your offense cycle; [See Chapter 9]
>
> (3) Plan for the time you no longer spend on your deviancy." [14]

The last item is particularly important for if I free up time from negative thinking, feeling, and behaving, it is necessary to fill that time with positive activities. Idleness can lead to boredom which can lead back to inappropriate thoughts, feelings, and behaviors.

There are a number of warning signs that can help us recognize that we may be slipping backwards towards old habits. We begin thinking of sexually charged incidents and perhaps start to fantasize about how "good" they made us feel; forgetting the hurt that may have been caused by our previous actions. This can occur more often when we are feeling down due to various negative events that may occur in our lives. There is also the "poor little old me" feeling we get when things don't seem to be going our way. We want to feel like we're in control of something. We may become frustrated and irritable—perhaps even blow up easily.

One of the strongest signs of slippage can be noted by thinking about the H.A.L.T. If we are Hungry (and not necessarily for food), Angry, Lonely, and Tired and stop taking care of ourselves we can develop an "I don't care" attitude—not just about ourselves but our job and other people as well. Broken record time again! If we aren't in touch with our thoughts, feelings, and behaviors, it is easy to let these warning signs take over and lead us down the wrong path thinking "just one more time" won't hurt. As with the alcoholic who has been dry for a while, taking one drink may lead him/her right back into their previous substance abuse state—so it can be with the sexual abuser/offender.

However, it's not necessary to go that route. If we have prepared a detailed Cycle and Relapse Prevention Plan, we have tools for change. And, as mentioned with the cycle we have prepared, we need to share the RPP with close family and friends who may recognize positive ideas that were missed. Also, they are not to be tucked away just because they have been finished. They are working tools. They need to be visible—out of sight; out of mind. They need to be referred to regularly to remind us of where we were—and don't want to be again—be it a prisoner of our own excesses or a prisoner of the state.

An effective RPP contains a number of items to consider. Below is a list of the most important ones and an explanation as to why they need to be considered. When working on your RPP, be sure to include all possible options you can think of. Being better prepared for the future is the only way to ensure a successful victim-free lifestyle. Though there are different approaches to RP, I view the following as the most comprehensive of others I've read about. Each of the 16 elements cited (taken from the NYS Sex Offender Program) are important; though some may carry more weight than others as individual situations/needs dictate. Review each element carefully and determine its importance to you:

1. Residence:

Where do you plan to live?

Whom do you plan on living with?

What is their relationship to you?

Are they aware of your sexual/abuse offending cycle/behavior?

Are there risky situations for you?

Keep in mind if you are a sex abuser/offender, you are not going to be a welcome sight in many places. Depending on the nature of your offense, living near schools, playgrounds, etc. may be forbidden. If you have sexually abused children, if returning to a family situation, are there children present? If so, even if they are your own, it may not be an acceptable living arrangement.

2. Employment:

Where do you plan on working?

What type of job(s)?

Will your employer know you are a sex abuser/offender?

If you do not have a job, what are some other alternatives?

Note: Working in jobs where there are potential victims, either as other employees or clientele, may not be possible.

3. Education:

Do you have a HS diploma/GED?

What do you plan to do to enhance your education?

4. Financial:

How will you meet your various expenses? Rent, food, clothes, etc?

5. Health:

How is your general health?

Will it prevent you from working?

6. Leisure:

How will you spend your free time?

Having completely idle time can be a negative because it allows you too much time for thinking—thoughts that can get you back into your cycle. And, of course, those leisure activities should be of a positive nature.

7. Addictions:

Do you have any addictions? If so, will you attend 12-step programs?

Do you know where and when they meet?

8. Personal relationships:

Who are they?

Are they healthy and supportive?

Do they know your sexual abuse/offending cycle/behavior?

That last question is important for it is necessary for those close to you to know about your cycle. Being close to you, they may notice subtle changes that you may be overlooking that could indicate you are slipping back into old habits. Will they be strong enough to call them to your attention?

9. Strengths:

What are your strong points?

What are you good at?

"Strength is having the power to get something done. Strength is not just about the power your muscles have to lift or move something. Strength also involves making a decision to do something and sticking with it. Strength is knowing what is right and doing it. Strength is about taking a stand for something you believe in, even when you are the only one willing do so. Strength requires hard work.

"It takes great strength to stay out of trouble. Using strength to face trouble can help you to stop causing harm. Strength helps you to stand tall and talk about trouble honestly. When you are able to take trouble you become stronger than it is. When you are confident in having the courage and strength to tackle trouble, you are able."[16]

10. Support System:

Counselors, pastors*, certain family members, parole officer, certain friends.

NOTE: Not everyone will make a good support partner. They need to be strong enough to tell what you NEED to hear not what you WANT to hear.

*If you are a convicted sex abuser/offender, being an active part of a church family may take time. You have to rebuild trust.

11. Issues Inventory:

What are some of the things you feel you'll need to continue working on? Self-esteem, isolation, stress, stuffing feelings, anger*, denial, abandonment, etc.?

*If you do not conquer your anger, it will have a negative effect on your entire RPP.

12. Environments to avoid:

   Obviously, if you are a sexual abuser/offender, there are various people/places/things you need to avoid. Consider these carefully as they may also impact on where you will be able to live and work.

13. Treatment:

   What types of treatment will you need to attend?

   Sex offender, 12-step, alcohol/drug/gambling counseling?

   Depression/psych counseling?

14. Short term goals:

   These are specific things you want to try to accomplish in the first one to three months after preparing your cycle and RP Plan.

15. Long term goals:

   These are things that you would like to accomplish a year or more away. Such as: have a steady job, have no more victims, etc.

16. Triggers:

> These are taken from your cycle and are those things that are important to try to avoid as they can start you off on your cycle.

- - - - - -

"There are three levels of sexual abuse prevention—primary, secondary and tertiary."[21]

1. Primary – "...to prevent sexual abuse before it occurs. Primary prevention puts the responsibility on the would-be abuser not to sexually abuse others." It "invites those who believe they have a sexual abuse problem to seek help and treatment, promoting a message of hope and recovery."

2. Secondary - "...to teach people how to avoid becoming a victim. [See Chapter 11]... Although crime prevention programs and efforts are valuable, secondary prevention programs place the responsibility for sexual abuse prevention on the potential victim."

3. Tertiary – "...to stop the abuse from continuing. This may involve treating victims of sexual abuse and teaching them ways to avoid and/or prevent

sexual abuse from happening again. Treating sexual abusers and helping them learn ways to not sexually abuse again is another form of tertiary prevention." ..."Prevention requires public education."[21]

This chapter and the previous one are the keys to regaining control of your life. Excessive sexual behavior can be very controlling. Sexual pleasure and fulfillment are things to enjoy—but they should not be dictating the way you live your life. And they definitely are not for the purpose of abusing/offending others.

Chapter 11

Recovery

"Honesty with oneself and others, self-acceptance that includes ones illness, and support for change by people who know the addiction's power to delude are prime determinants of recovery."

Patrick Carnes, PhD

"Recovery! Why do I need recovery? I know what I did was wrong; it won't happen again. I made some bad choices, but does that make me a sex addict—or out of control with my sexual urges?" No, not necessarily. Do these questions have a familiar ring to them? I hope so. I asked myself those questions over and over again. The only thing I thought I had to recover from was making poor sexual choices. However, my actions caused much pain (emotional and/or physical) to myself, victims, and extended victims. I needed to take a long hard look at myself—my actions and my attitude towards sex—and rethink them in light of what has been presented in the preceding chapters. If we can see ourselves in any of the information presented, and it is quite obvious I did, it is time to take a deeper look at our attitude towards sex and sexual feelings over all. For if we don't get a handle on why we did what we did, there is a fair chance we could abuse/offend or do it again.

When I started the Sex Offender Program during my incarceration, I still saw my inappropriate sexual behavior towards my victims as somewhat of an isolated incident. I expressed it as "under my roof, under my control." How often would I have under age females in my home? I also felt that my situation was unique because of my education and community status. However, once I started reading books on the subject of sexual abuse/offending, and specifically on sexual addiction, I had to ask myself, "Did the writers follow me around and get inside my head?" or were there, in fact, others like me? Obviously the latter is the logical choice. I was in prison and in the Sex Offender Program and at various times with me was a Baptist minister, school teacher, rabbi, and other highly educated individuals. The books by Carnes and Schaumburg mentioned earlier were particularly helpful in identifying long standing thoughts, feelings, and behaviors that led to my sexual offending and my self-declared status of sex addict. By the way, I have no doubt that had my actions not been reported and my later arrest, my behavior would have gotten worse. I had lost control of my life.

It wasn't, however, until my counselor told me I "degraded and humiliated women," and my wife's agreement with that assessment, that I really had to stop and take a deep look at all my sexual encounters and came to the conclusion, as I said before, they were all about me—my satisfaction; my sexual gratification wants. It was a bitter pill to swallow, but one that made me examine my attitude towards women and my sexual experiences over all. As a result of that examination, I recognized that just to understand myself was not enough. It was essential that I adopt a whole different attitude; and that doesn't happen overnight. It is an on-going process; hence, the term "recovery." I must "recover" from my negative sexual mindset towards the female gender and the overall sexual experience to a more positive one. If I don't remember my old thoughts, feelings, and behaviors that caused my inappropriate acting out, I could be doomed to make the same wrong choices again. That is, as I see it, the importance of making recovery a lifetime process. I was, unfortunately, late in doing so, and at the insistence of my wife, sought professional counseling to turn my negative sexual attitude into a positive, wholesome one, but that was short-lived due to my pending incarceration. However, it was continued in prison and after being released.

Later, while incarcerated, I was introduced to Sex Addicts Anonymous (S.A.A.), one of four Twelve-Step programs that address inappropriate (or excessive) sexual behavior, in the same manner that AA addresses alcoholism. They had developed a self-assessment questionnaire by which I could view myself in regards to my sexual behavior/attitude. (See questionnaire at the end of this chapter.) "If you answer `yes` to more than one of these questions, we encourage you to seek out additional literature as a resource or attend an S.A.A. meeting to further assess your need."[19] The test does not prove one way or another if one is a sex addict but it certainly should put up warning flags. As for me, I could say yes to ten of the twelve questions. Problem? You bet! Again, I remind you that not all sex abusers/offenders are sex addicts. The information on sex addiction is mentioned as a tool to aid in your personal sexual assessment. It took that incarceration to really drive the point home that I had a serious problem. It also was necessary for me to continue counseling while incarcerated to aid in my understanding. It was a requirement of parole as well when I was released.

In his book, **Sexuality in Perspective**, Jean V. addresses his recovery from sexual addiction. He observed that "Sex has to become *optional* for us sex addicts."[18] It is a matter of retraining our thoughts from a "must have" view of sex to one of "I can survive without it." He goes on to say, and the same applies to me, "I was married and had a partner with whom to practice sex, thus never seriously considered that sex might need to be optional for me. ... The challenge was obvious. To progress in recovery, I had to surrender and accept sex as totally optional in my life."[18] If I can surrender sex as a "must have" part of my life, the better chance I'll have of reducing my addictive tendencies and work towards positive recovery. On the other hand, if I can't put my sexual wants in check, the chance that I will relapse increases. It is not necessary to give up sex as an expression of a total love commitment (though for some it may be necessary). What is essential is knowing and understanding what the sexual experience really means to you _and_ your partner—and that is paramount to the recovery process. I cannot think of sex as an entitlement—it is not. If I do, it will weaken my recovery and may lead to my reoffending. "Once we have a solid footing in recovery, we cease treating people as objects and instead treat them as equals deserving our respect."[18] I now spend more time doing things with and for my wife than I ever did before—she deserves the positive attention after years of neglect. We also have discovered a special intimacy that places no demands on either party other than unconditional love. Intimacy is an often misunderstood word. It usually conjures up thoughts of sex, but that is not the sole meaning of it. It is the closeness and appreciation of each other's individuality that is ultimately important for a full and loving relationship.

Jean V. noted, "...I had feared that practicing sexual abstinence would involve agonizing periods of sexual obsession while craving an orgasm."[18] To his surprise, and mine, this did not happen. He believed his biological programming required a sexual release several times each week. He had previously become tense and irritable whenever not experiencing orgasms regularly. However, during his period of abstinence he learned that his level of sexual desire was directly related to the degree that he did or did not entertain sexual thoughts. I had the same experience. His *willingness* to surrender these thoughts determined whether he would experience serenity or whether he would be tormented by sexual obsessions. His bottom line: "If I am having difficulty abstaining from sexual behaviors, I am *choosing* to generate my sexual drive through indulging in sexual intrigue. Intrigue that is mentally nurtured, sparks obsessions which when entertained long enough generate compulsions."[18] I couldn't have said it better myself. I was driven by the short-lived euphoric feeling of ejaculation that appeared to wash away my stress. I did not take into account the guilt and shame my actions placed on me until sometime later. I simply blamed the external forces I allowed to control me, as well as my personal inner thoughts and feelings, as my stress producers.

> "Intimacy is as transient as stable, as simple as complex, as forgettable as memorable,

and as shallow as profound. It is worth great effort, yet great effort drives it away. Intimacy is one of life's greatest joys yet must be replenished or the joy is lost. Intimacy is a fact. Intimacy is a riddle. Intimacy is a gift—one we give ourselves yet can only be received by us when given to another."[18]

What a profound statement and definition of the purest form of intimacy.

It is, therefore, necessary to take the concepts presented in the previous chapters to heart. See where they fit in your life. I know I had to. Chapters 9 and 10 are particularly crucial for, if done correctly, they will outline the areas (thoughts, feelings, and behaviors) that need to be worked on to rid oneself of negative sexual behaviors that can lead to offending or re-offending. It is not enough just to be familiar with the concepts of the cycle and relapse prevention; it is essential to spend a lot of time in understanding and developing them. It is also important, as I mentioned before, to have the cycle and prevention plan reviewed by someone else. We seldom see ourselves as others see us. It takes others to see our faults—<u>and us to be open to their comments</u>.

As noted in the Relapse Prevention Plan in Chapter 10, I had to identify sixteen areas considered essential to preventing a relapse and lead to recovery. Remember, I consider myself sexually addicted. Therefore, recognizing that there is no cure, I had to develop the willingness to control my urges! I must remain ever vigilant to my thoughts, feelings, and behaviors. To help me with that I need support. To that end there are two specific areas of the Relapse Prevention Plan that are a must: My Personal Relationships and My Support System.

<u>Personal Relationships:</u>   These are close family members and friends. I am most fortunate to have a wife who loves me unconditionally. She is familiar with both depression and addictive behavior and is not afraid to tell me if she notices me in a down mood or slipping into old habits (many of which demeaned her). The most important part for me was being able to accept constructive criticism where before I often did not. For that matter, I didn't take criticism very well at all. Thankfully, my son has reestablished his relationship with

me despite it being a family member who was one of my victims. My sister and her daughter have also maintained a positive relationship as have several friends from the past. I am also fortunate to have reestablished a positive and proper relationship with the family member I abused. Little by little I am reestablishing positive relationships with other family members and past friends and associates. It is a slow but positive process.

Support System: Many of those with whom I reestablished a relationship have also become part of my support system by showing love and concern. My psychologist and group and individual therapy counselors have been extremely helpful in continuing to help me see myself as I should be. Yet they have, at the same time encouraged me to continue looking at those factors that could pose a high risk for me so I will remember to avoid them. I have also established contact with a 12-Step group. Along with the help of medication and the training and reading that has been available to me, I am now able to see my offending behavior more clearly and all the hurt it has caused. I have also been encouraged to do this writing as a means of solidifying my understanding of what I did and its overall impact. It has been very helpful for me and I hope it will be helpful to you the reader.

One area that I felt was going to be hard to seek support from was the religious community—and I was right. Some people deal with spirituality by looking within themselves or looking to their own perception of a higher power rather than being bound to a specific denomination. I needed clergy support! And although I did receive it from several clergy friends, the pastor from my home church as well as the denomination headquarters failed to respond to me. I felt rejected and, as previously noted, morally and spiritually bankrupt.

Several months after my release to parole, I took a chance and stopped by the small community church of the denomination I felt rejected me. I met with the pastor who, despite having a previous appointment, saw or felt my need and took me under his wing. He listened to my story and welcomed me in Christian fellowship—praying with and for me. Do I attend church? At the time of my initial writing, no. At least not at the church that I wanted to attend for all are not as understanding, compassionate, forgiving, and loving as their pastor—and I accepted that, reluctantly. It has taken time, over two years, but I was finally allowed to attend a small country church with few youth that my then pastor also served. Several members of the church were made aware of my status yet received me warmly. I have to prove myself worthy all over again. I can say now, that I have received permission to attend the church of my choice. It took time, but I no longer feel morally and spiritually bankrupt. The hand of Christian fellowship has been extended to me. I am a living, breathing person. I did a terrible thing, but I am worth saving. Perhaps, as my former pastor noted, there may be a ministry of a sort in store for me. Only time will tell.

Professional counseling, 12-step groups, and other therapeutic programs are available to help those of us who have let our lives get out of control and fall prey to the lure of sexual urges. Don't be afraid to seek help before it is too late—or too late AGAIN! And don't give up on whatever program(s) you become part of. The longer the involvement, the more you learn; the more you learn, the more positive your life may become. And just as important, others may learn from us and help them gain or regain control over their lives. I know there are times when I feel I have "gotten the message" and don't want to relive my actions any more. But I also know that is the wrong attitude. I need to face the "demons" of my life so I can control them rather than the other way around. You are not alone. I found help; you can too. I credit my pastor for comparing sexual excessiveness—addiction, if you will—to being trapped in quicksand. The more you struggle <u>alone</u> to get out of it, the deeper and deeper you go into it. The analogy holds true for any form of addiction. And the key word is "alone." It is extremely rare to break a long standing pattern of behavior by oneself. "Unfortunately, sexual abuse is a complex problem that requires more than willpower and simple punitive solutions."[21] It takes knowledge, tools, and the <u>desire</u> to change our previous way of living.

"Take your time and seriously think about your life and what it means to you. Don't cut yourself short by discounting the chance to help yourself. Don't make up convenient excuses in order to avoid looking at yourself. Even if you are not sure of what you want, you have nothing to lose by trying. Most importantly, be sure to give being in treatment a fair chance and your best effort."[7]   It is not always easy but it is worth it in the long run. Facing our sexual excesses and all the harm they may have caused can make us want to back away from treatment in an effort to put what we did behind us. Unfortunately, the old adage that says if you forget (or ignore) the past, you are doomed to repeat it, has been found too true. "To change your life you can't just change the bad behavior; you must learn to change how you think [and feel and behave]."[9]   I can certainly attest to that!

I can not undo what I did. I can only go forward from this point and hope that I can use my experience and "sexual rebirth" for good. I have to live with what I did as do my victims. In an article in the Sunday (Schenectady, NY) Gazette, August 20, 2006, concerning a convicted rapist, he stated. "I literally kick myself…every day. It hurts. It hurts a lot. As much as I pray, as much as I work on it in counseling, I still can't repair the pain that I caused a girl, her family, my family, my kids. It's very hard to deal with…" Such feeling can only come from honestly grasping the negative impact of inappropriate sexual behavior.

"Success or failure is not an accident, it is deliberate. There are specific things that you have to do in order to succeed and there are specific things you have to do in order to fail. You may ask, "What are they?"

1.   The type of *belief* (interest, values, morals) [you have].

2.   The type of *thinking* (ideas and thoughts of self, family, community and life) [you have].

3.   The type of *attitude* (patience/impatience, determination/indetermination) [you display].

4.   The type of *association* (right minded people, right minded places, right minded activities/wrong minded people, wrong minded places, wrong minded activities)[you have with others].

5.   The degree of *courage* to think (to constructively criticize self, rethink everything)"[8]

It will be a struggle to defeat those unproductive, disregardful, reckless, and self-defeating thoughts that project an inferior self-image. "We must live where we think! If our 'home' of thinking is in disorder, our life will be in disorder; however, if our 'home' of thinking is in order, our life will be in order. Order lends itself to progress and establishment. Disorder lends itself to regression and disability."[8]

TWELVE QUESTIONS FOR SELF-ASSESSMENT[19]

1.   Do you keep secrets about your sexual or romantic activities from those important to you? Do you lead a double life?   Yes__ No____

2.   Have your needs driven you to have sex in places or with people you would not normally choose?
Yes__ No____

3.   Do you find yourself looking for sexually arousing articles or scenes in newspapers, magazines or other media?   Yes__ No___

4.   Do you find that romantic or sexual fantasies interfere with your relationship or are preventing you from facing problems?   Yes__ No__

5.   Do you frequently want to get away from a sex partner after having sex? Do you frequently feel remorse, shame, or guilt after a sexual encounter? Yes__ No____

6.   Do you feel shame about your body or your sexuality, such that you avoid touching your body or engaging in sexual relationships? Do you fear that you have no sexual feelings, that you are asexual?   Yes__ No__

7.   Does each new relationship continue to have the same destructive patterns which prompted you to leave the last relationship?   Yes__ No__

8.   Is it taking more variety and frequency of sexual and romantic activities than previously to bring the same levels of excitement and relief?   Yes__ No__

9. Have you been arrested or are you in danger of being arrested because of your practices of voyeurism, exhibitionism, prostitution, sex with minors, indecent phone call, etc.?   Yes__ No__

10. Does your pursuit of sex or romantic relationships interfere with your spiritual beliefs or development?
                                                    Yes__ No__

11. Do your sexual activities include the risk, threat, or reality of disease, pregnancy, coercion or violence?
                                                    Yes__ No__

12. Has your sexual or romantic behavior ever left you feeling hopeless, alienated from others, or suicidal?
                                                    Yes__ No__

Reprinted with permission from ISO of SAA, P.O. Box 700949, Houston, TX   77270

Chapter 12

"No More Victims"

"Having no more victims is the only measure of whether you are being successful [in your recovery]."

Robert Longo et al

How do we change the public's perception of the sex abuser/offender? The simplest answer is, "We don't!" At least, not with the current legal system and the media's perception of all sex offenders. Sexual offending is a heinous crime regardless of what is done. People have been victimized—and far too often these people are children! It falls upon each abuser/offender to prove he/she is worthy to be accepted back into society. That process will not be an easy one—nor will it always be a successful one. It will take time, courage, and determination on the part of the recovering abuser/offender—and a lot of personal support and a more educated public. There are organizations working to that end.

The ultimate aim of a sex offender program is, of course, to reduce the number of sex offenses carried out by abusers/offenders. It will not be an easy task either. Unfortunately, there are many sex offenders and potential sex offenders in communities across the country that have not yet been caught. Obviously, sexual offending therapy, though proven to have a positive effect and has contributed significantly to the smaller sexual re-offending rate compared to other types of crimes, does not address the potential, or undiscovered, abuser/offender. It will take the education of our children and the reeducation of families and individuals, and communities as a whole, as to their obligation to teach proper sexual values. Perhaps all who are sentenced to jail/prison time should be exposed in some degree to a sex offender program. Maybe they have not committed such a crime directly, but because of their attitude, it could happen next time. At least empathy training should be required—along with anger management. A federal study has shown that sex offenders who receive treatment, have a much lower rate of recidivism (repeat offending) than those who commit other crimes. Most often, if a sex offender is rearrested, it is for a crime other than a sexual one.

It stands to reason that if you have gotten this far you read my sexual bio in Chapter 1 and the various topic summarizations of the Sex Offender Program I attended. It should be obvious that the three key words are **thoughts, feelings, and behaviors**. To these can be added a fourth word: **choice**. In the long run, despite the urges that build up that could lead to acting out, it is ultimately our choice to do so. Each holds an important place in most of the chapters—and cannot be stressed enough. I can only hope that reading this gives some idea of the serious impact sexual abusing/offending/excessiveness has on the individual victim(s) and society as a whole.

If you have not experienced it first hand, sex abusers/offenders are looked down on by society—and with good reason. Although it portrays, perhaps, an extreme reaction to a sex offender moving into a neighborhood, the movie, **The Man Next Door**, is something to see. It captures well the emotions, the feelings of people who fear having their lives, their families, exposed to such abusers/offenders. Many of the emotions and feelings expressed have been echoed in newspaper articles about sex abusers/offenders moving into neighborhoods across the country. In some instances it appears to border on the panic. Such an attitude makes it extremely difficult for a sex abuser/offender to transition back into society, develop meaningful relationships, and find employment to support himself/herself and family so as not to become either a societal burden or a re-offender of sex or other crimes because he/she is not accepted in the community. As it is, it is often very difficult for a convicted abuser/offender to find an appropriate and decent place to live with or without his family.

"A sex offender who is confronted with his offense by the victim, the legal system, his congregation, friends, or family is not helped by being ostracized. This only furthers his isolation and hostility, which makes it difficult for him to try to change. He is not helped by being the focus of vengeful attacks, verbal or physical. [Or by a judicial/penal system that does little to understand and aid the correction of inappropriate sexual behavior.] A group of people who are willing to be supportive, to strengthen his resolve to stay in a treatment program, to be present with him through the process of change is what is most needed."[10] (Emphasis added.)

That is why the support system emphasized in Chapters 10 and 11 is so important to establish.

I have used a lot of reference material in putting this together and quoted extensively from them. My reason for doing so is that what the authors have said is far better than what I could have come up with for many of them are experts in their field. More importantly, what they said had a significant impact on me and helped me see the "me that was" and led me to the "me that should have been." The quotes I have used really spoke to me or emphasized a point I was attempting to make. I can only hope that what I have compiled and put down can help even one person see the error of their ways and turn away from excessive sexual thoughts, feelings, and behaviors, or at least help them see themselves in a different light after abusing/offending or not doing it again. Besides what I have used, there is a wealth of studies and other written works concerning sexual abuse/offending/excessiveness. Most of the attached list of references provides a wealth of information on the subject.

One point I hope I have made abundantly clear. Though Chapter 1 talks of the way my thoughts of sexual relationships developed, they are no excuse for my actions. Nor was my path to my sexual abusing/offending the only way one comes to those actions. Each abuser/offender has his/her own story. Regrettably, few have taken the time to tell their story to others in the hopes of preventing further sexual abuse/offending. **There are no excuses for what I did!** I was educated; I was by many standards a moralist. Yet I CHOSE to sexually offend because all I cared about in the realm of sexual relations was me; though I had convinced myself that I was pleasing to the females I had been with. I am truly sorry for all the hurt I have caused and I, as well as my victims, will remember the offending behavior for a long time. I can only hope the lessons I have learned, and summarized in the text, will prevent someone else from being victimized—and a potential offender to seek help before it is too late. **Don't make the same wrong choice that I did!**

You have read how one can develop into a sexual abuser/offender and how to stop, or at least reduce, the chance that that will happen. It is also important to take a look at what can be done to minimize the chances of a sexual offense happening if for no other reason than to consider ways to protect yourself and your own family. In her book, *Sexual Violence, The Unmentionable Sin*, Marie Marshall Fortune makes a case for ending sexual violence by highlighting three "p's":

> "***Precautions*** are steps taken to minimize or avoid potential dangers; ***protection*** includes steps taken when someone is faced with immediate danger; and ***prevention*** describes activity to address the danger at its roots and to eliminate it. Precautions, protection, and prevention are strategies that are implemented by persons working both individually and collectively."[10] (Emphasis added.)

Although the 3 p's, as Fortune defines them, are primarily designed to make individuals aware of what they can do to reduce their chance of being a victim of sexual abuse/offending, they can also be applied to the potential (or actual) abuser/offender.

Precautions: Once the cycle and relapse prevention plan has been completed, you have taken a major step in understanding how to avoid situations that could lead to abuse/offending because you are equipped to recognize slippage into old habits. It is helpful to have readily available phone numbers of family members and friends that can be called should you find inappropriate thoughts and feelings starting to overwhelm you. It would also be helpful to prepare a pocket size relapse prevention card to refer to if other means of support aren't readily available. Of course the supporting individual should be ones with whom you have shared your cycle and relapse prevention plan so they can more readily understand your need for a neutral party to help break the chain of thoughts and feelings that could cause an acting out situation.

Protection: This step includes the above but also considers steps to be taken when faced with an immediate situation that could lead to acting out. Such actions might be to immediately leave the situation you are in, shouting "NO" if necessary, spilling something on yourself, and other things that will break your inappropriate thought pattern. One of the best ways is to be around others engaged in some positive activity: sports, theater, lunch/dinner with family or friends where, hopefully, the mind becomes absorbed in a positive group activity and is drawn away from negative thoughts and feelings that could lead to trouble.

Prevention: This "...describes activity to address the danger and eliminate it."[10]   Here is a good area to apply "self-talk" and other "safety" methods that can interrupt the negative train of thought and feelings that could have a significant impact on ones freedom and self-esteem. Avoiding such people, places, and/or things that have helped fuel the fires of inappropriate sexual behavior in the past should be high on the list. Remind oneself that the intended victim is someone's loved family member. Also, the possibility of arrest, imprisonment, embarrassment of self and family, and negative financial impact, are just a few of the things that can be used. Even turning over car keys to someone can prevent the idle driving around to see what's "out there."

As mentioned in the previous chapters, it is equally important when purging ones' mind of negative trends, to have positive back up plans. Simply to stop negative actions is not enough for that frees up time. If you don't have a plan to use that new time for something useful it becomes a "plan" for failure in your acting out prevention.

As cited earlier, the whole purpose of this presentation is an attempt to create "**No More Victims.**" All the promises to oneself and/or to others that we will not abuse/offend, or that there will not be a recurrence of previous inappropriate sexual behaviors mean nothing if even one more person falls victim to sexual abusing/offending because of our actions.

One Last Word

Being a sex offender/abuser has additional ramifications beyond incarceration, registering, and the social stigma assigned to us. There are also various restrictions such as where you can live and work. A "looking over your shoulder" feeling is also part of the price we pay for our actions. We spend a lot of time wondering who knows about us and what they may say or do. Over time that feeling will subside but it is important to keep a log of your whereabouts (time left, destination(s), and return mileage).

It can happen that if there is a sex offense in your community and no person is immediately a suspect, authorities can call you in for questioning so you need to be able to prove your innocence. If you are someone with sexual issues that could result in incarceration if caught, the same applies to you. You never know when someone is going to report you. I was called out twice by two different police agencies that said I was ID'd as someone trying to pick up young girls. My being able to prove I couldn't have been in the areas mentioned saved the day.

So be wise, be sober, and above all be well. I hope the contents of this book will support you in your recovery. Take what you want and leave the rest. If you are having similar problems as I faced, it could lead to incarceration or worse.

Bibliography

1. **False Intimacy**, by Harry W. Schaumburg, PhD, NavPress, 1997

2. **Contrary to Love—Helping the Sexual Addict**, by Patrick Carnes, PhD, Hazelden, 1994

3. **The Four Agreements**, by Dr. Don Miguel Ruiz, Amber-Allen Publishing Co,   1997

4. **Out of the Shadows—Understanding Sexual Addiction**, by Patrick Carnes, PhD, Hazelden, 1983

5. **Don't Call It Love—Recovery from Sexual Addiction,** by Patrick Carnes, PhD, Bantam Books, 1991

6. **Healing the Shame That Binds You**, by John Bradshaw

7. **Who Am I And Why Am I In Treatment?** By Robert Freeman-Longo and Laren Bays, NEARI Press (2006) (Whitman Distribution, P. O. Box 1156, Lebanon, NH 03766)

8. Oneida (NY) Correctional Facility Sex Offender Program curriculum. The program is a compilation of information from various sources.

9. **Why Did I Do It Again?** See No. 7 above. (2000)

10. **Sexual Violence, The Unmentionable Sin**,
    by Marie Marshall Fortune, The Pilgrim Press,
    1983

11. Source Unknown

12. **Empathy and Compassionate Action,** See
    No. 7 Above. (2000)

13. **Parade**, February 19, 2006, "Let's Fight This
    Terrible Crime Against Our Children," by
    Andrew Vachss

14. **How Can I Stop?** See No. 7 Above. (2000)

15. **Facing the Shadows,** by Barbara K. Schwartz,
    PhD and Gregory M. S. Canfield, MSW, Civic
    Research Institute, Inc., 1996

16. **The T.O.P. (Trauma Outcome Process)
    Workbook,** by Joann Schladale, MS, LMFT,
    Resources for Resolving Violence, 2002

17. **Juvenile Sexual Offending**, by Gail Ryan and
    Sandy Lane, Editors, Jossey-Bass, 1997

18. **Sexuality In Perspective – A Story of
    Recovery from Sex Addiction and View on
    Healthy Sexuality,** by Jean V., Valjean
    Publishing, 1998

19. **ISO OF SAA, Inc.,** Houston, TX

20. **Empathy In Sex Offenders,** by W. L.

Marshall, S. M. Hudson, R. Jones, and Yolanda M. Fernandez, Clinical Psychology Review, Vol. 15, No. 2

21. **Sexual Abuse in America: Epidemic of the 21st century,** by Robert E. Freeman-Longo and Geral T. Blanchard, The Safer Society Press, 1998

22. **Heal Your Self-Esteem—The 10 Principles of Healing,** by Bryan Robinson

Special Note: For those desiring to look further into sex addiction consider, the following:

Circle of Life - The Process of Sexual Recovery (a 12 Step workbook by KJ Nivin) at
http://www.amazon.com/-/e/B0043TC2O6

ABOUT THE AUTHOR

Writing as S. Sands, the author comes from a loving, but basically single parent home as his father passed away shortly after he turned ll. He was subsequently raised by his mother, maiden aunt, and sister. That upbringing did play a subtle part in the development of his sexual attitude.

He joined the Navy and had his first sexual experience in Japan and, looking back, was a bit traumatized by it. Although tempted a number of times, did not have sexual contact again until he married some six years later. However, in those intervening years, he became more and more exposed to a variety of pornography which, it turned out, greatly shaped his sexual attitude even further and, regrettably, not in a good way. His first marriage failed due in large part to his tainted view of sex derived from his pornographic usage and very nearly did in his second.

Upon retiring from the Navy, he returned to his home state and held various employments and did extensive volunteer work in many fine organizations, including his church. Despite all the positive influence of the organizations and his church, he still could not break the hold that pornography had on him. He continued to delve into inappropriate sexual activities finally culminating in the charges that placed him in prison.

During his time in prison and through the Sex Offender Program offered, he found what he considered to be the roots of his sexual behavior. With that knowledge he worked the program with a greater sense of understanding how he came to be where he was. During this time he also discovered the writings of Dr. Patrick Carnes, PhD and quickly identified with them and was able to define himself as a sex addict. Since his release he has been involved in Sex Addicts Anonymous to work the 12-Step program for his benefit and hopefully for the benefit of others.

The reason this small book came about was through his trying to find personal stories of those who struggled with sexual issues and how they came to understand them and work on overcoming them in a positive way. Mostly he found scholarly works. Though helpful, he felt they lacked the down-to-earth approach that he felt was needed. Taking his experiences and the prison program he participated in, along with his numerous readings, he applied the lessons learned and came up this with timely book. The book shows the path he took that led him to his personal downfall and eventual recovery. He hopes that those that read the book will see a little of themselves in it and the direction they are headed if they do not change their sexual attitude.